THE CONVERT

... the pinnacle of God's love ...

M.J. MATUKA

authorHOUSE®

AuthorHouse™ UK
1663 Liberty Drive
Bloomington, IN 47403 USA
www.authorhouse.co.uk
Phone: 0800.197.4150

Published by AuthorHouse 11/08/2016

ISBN: 978-1-5246-6502-9 (sc)
ISBN: 978-1-5246-6503-6 (hc)
ISBN: 978-1-5246-6501-2 (e)

Print information available on the last page.

Luke: 8-10

"Or suppose a woman who has ten silver coins loses one of them – what does she do? She lights a lamp, sweeps her house, and **looks carefully everywhere until she finds it**. When she finds it, she calls her friends and neighbors together and say to them, 'I am so happy I found the coin I lost. Let us celebrate!' In the same way, **I tell you, the angels of God rejoice over one sinner who repents."**

Table of Contents

Preface

Let us pray!

"Our Heavenly Father, May your Name be honored. May Your Kingdom come; may your Will be done on earth as it is in heaven". We thank you for giving us your eternal gift – Your only begotten Son, to be our sole hope of mercy. We are thankful to realize your immeasurable love to us, and your jealousy, which grows every moment to see us repented. We therefore pray for your mercy to surpass your anger because of our sinful nature – and help us reach a point whereby we may be sanctified and made righteous before your eyes. We humbly ask these in the name of your Son Jesus Christ, Amen!

* * *

The passion I have for the new Converts into the Kingdom of God to write this book is based on the foundation that can be laid into their faith to bring about the lasting consequences. The Convert is the basis of the display of the Love of God manifested in the reason to present Jesus Christ as the Savior and Lord in their lives.

Acknowledgements

I dedicate the whole work to God Almighty, the Holy one of Israel!

Also special thanks to my family, which is always behind me in pursuing this work to make it a success. Thanks to all my brothers and sisters in fellowship to Christ; all the intercessors worldwide; all men of God in leadership and you the reader; thank you and may God richly bless you and fulfill all the good desires of your heart to the glory of His name!

Thanks to Mr Litelu T.J., Mr Morajane D.E., Mr Mokoena M.M., Mr Kolokome S.P. and Mrs Tshabalala D.M. – may the Lord embrace you in His Love forever!

Note: Jesus loves you!

Chapter 1

"Do You Love Me?"

Love is somewhat, a very tricky subject to talk about because it is something, which involves feelings and emotions. Such emotions are better understood in expressions and actions than in mere talking. Love in its merit is a bond, which involves time, sacrifice, sharing, commitment, dedication and truth-value on someone who loves. It is better understood by the person who loves and become demonstrated to the one who is loved in order to express what is within the emotional sphere of the lover. The fact of it being an emotion or a feeling qualifies it to be a subset of the 'Soul' as a part of "Man."

Love is good, but may turn bad and die if it is not well grounded. The grounding aspect of love, in the context of this book, defines the difference between 'God as love' and the type of love credited for men. However, God displayed who He is for human beings on the cross of Calvary and that display is what is termed 'true love.' I have included, in this chapter, a brief description of what might be necessary for Christians to keep the 'Love' and fellowship burning more and more based on the following scripture:

* * *

John 21: 15 – 17
After they had eaten, Jesus said to Simon Peter," Simon son of John, do you love me more than these others do?" "Yes Lord," he answered, "you know that I love you." Jesus said to him, "take care of my lambs." A second time Jesus said to him, "Simon son of John, "do you love me?" "Yes Lord," he answered, "you know that I love you." Jesus said to him, "Take care of my sheep." A third time Jesus said, "Simon son of John, do you love me?" Peter was sad because Jesus asked him the third time, "Do you love me?" so he said to Him, "Lord you know everything; you know that I love you!" Jesus said to him, "Take care of my sheep."

The conversation of Jesus and the Peter in the scripture above, makes one to pause a moment and try to get to understand the in-depth of their discussion. It looks like Peter struggled to get to the deepest connotation of the question asked by Jesus. The repetition of the question might imply that Peter was short of understanding to the meaning of the question in this case, or that Jesus wanted to emphasize its meaning until well interpreted in Peter's mind.

Peter had been a disciple to Jesus for a period of about three years since the beginning of the ministry, and he surely anticipated the Lord's sayings and believed to be used to them. Unfortunately, in this case, the question was more than it could be anticipated. It was only at the third time that Peter began to organize his mind and try to digest around the meaning of the question. I believe the sadness he endured penetrated to the deepest ends of his imagination and made him understand the question exactly as posed to him. What would you say, or how would you react when your Master repeatedly asks you one question for several times as if your answer is not accepted or else doubted? Especially after such an incident of Jesus brutal death on the cross, remember that the very same Peter was prophesied to deny knowing Jesus three times before the cock crowed.

"Do you love me?" In true sense, this question is too much difficult to approach because it is not enough to simply, say, "Yes you know that I love you." It may be easy to say it out but may be so difficult to prove and keep it as a lasting promise.

Peter consented to a lifetime responsibility by his affirmation to love Jesus. He was appointed in principle among the disciples to carry the responsibility of seeing to it that, the gospel of Jesus is preached, and that more disciples are being recruited.

How would he start ministering and establishing more disciples when it was so tense in the City? The gospel of Jesus was declared a blasphemy and any one who would be caught preaching about His name was to be arrested.

Acts 9:13 – 14
Ananias answered, "Lord, many people have told me about this man and about all the terrible things he has done to your people in Jerusalem. And he has come to Damascus with authority from the chief priests to arrest all who worship you."

The answer to this question goes no further than the mention of the presence of the Holy Spirit to purposefully, further the intentions of the Lord. Just after they received the Holy Spirit in them, they came out of the place where they were gathered and begin to minister in tongues that everyone gathered around as a spectator would understand them in his/her native language, and that was the beginning. The Lord made it easy for them by sending the Holy Spirit to give them power and to break the fearful and somewhat icy atmosphere which was prevailing, and let them boldly out to the open where they must go and minister the Gospel.

From the scripture in the book of John above, three distinctions, which Jesus made, spelled out exactly the responsibilities of the Apostle Peter as a point of departure in his charge-ship over the church. However, Jesus wanted to emphasize to Peter and to ascertain that he should really consider the safety and welfare of the souls. Let us unpack these directives so that we may understand:

The first Directive

"Take care of my lambs"

In some of His teachings in the Bible, Jesus used to utter parables. The knowledge about Him using parables infers that the reference in the scripture above refer the lambs as the people worldwide who are the chosen but are still lost and suffer bondage. They are the ones who still need to be ministered for and told about the Good News of salvation, so that they may repent. These are the siblings, who still need to be fed with milk and be nurtured for their faith in Christ (1 Peter 2: 2). They need to be guided with love in their disbelief, to accept Jesus Christ as their Lord and Savior.

The second Directive

"Take care of my sheep"

The 'sheep' in the first place refers to Christ disciples at large, meaning all the people whose faith is Christian based irrespective of their degree of growth in the body of Christ. They are the followers who are humbly submissive and looking forward to inheriting the Kingdom of heaven. They also, need to be nurtured and guided with love until they attain full growth so that none of them may be lost, but be retained and functional as people who will draw many more in the discipleship as well.

The third Directive

The 'sheep' in the second place refers to the twelve disciples chosen by Jesus to establish His companion. Peter was to see to it that their faith did not wear off but to strengthen them to endure more tribulations that might come their way. They were meant to role model the way in the true Christian life in joy and in hardship. From their spirit shall other people of the same instincts be born in order to perfect the saints! Moreover, these shall inherit the gifts of the Spirit to accomplish the Will of God. They are those who form a cluster in the ministerial gifts of the Holy Spirit even today (*Ephesians 4: 11*).

Luke 22:32
But I have prayed for you, Simon that your faith will not fail. And when you turn back to me, you must strengthen your brothers

At one point Jesus said to Peter:

Matthew 16:18
"And so I tell you, Peter, **you are a rock**, and on this rock foundation I will build my church, and not even death will ever be able to overcome it. I will give you the keys of the kingdom of heaven; what you prohibit on earth will be prohibited in heaven, and what you permit on earth will be permitted in heaven."

It is as if Peter pronounced his reply to the question in a much fleshly way than he had to pronounce it spiritually. This shows that he actually ran short of understanding as far as his responsibilities extends. The little he could anticipate in mind was that his span of duty is limited only to his kinship, whereas the Lord wanted to conciliate between Him and the entire lost humanity.

It took the Lord a moment to vividly reveal to Peter the actual meaning of His Will about the lost. Let us check the following scripture:

Acts 10:11-15
He saw heaven opened and something coming down that looked like a large sheet being lowered by its four corners to the earth. In it were all kinds of animals, reptiles and wild birds. A voice said to him, "Get up, Peter, kill and eat!" But Peter said, "Certainly not, Lord! I have never eaten anything ritually unclean or defiled." The voice spoke to him again, "Do not consider anything unclean that God has declared clean." This happened three times, and the thing was taken back up into heaven.

Peter's vision seemed unclear to him until the Holy Spirit directed him to abide (verse 20 – "so get ready and go down, and do not hesitate to go with them, for I have sent them.") and Cornelius explained it all. Cornelius was just a mere captain, a gentile by the way, who according to Peter and the other disciples was not supposed to inherit righteousness in any way. It was only in verse 34 – 35 that his understanding was confessed.

Acts 10:34-35
Peter began to speak: "**I now realize that it is true that God treats everyone on the same basis**. Those who worship him and do what is right are acceptable to him, no matter what race they belong to. You know the message He sent to the people of Israel, proclaiming the Good News of peace through Jesus Christ, who is Lord of all."

Peter went along with them and ministered, and thereafter became shocked by the way they received the gospel and baptismal with the Holy Spirit. He began to realize that the love of God is not centered on some isolated group of people, but extents beyond individual span of imagination. The experience he endured at Caesarea undoubtedly paved the way for the full acceptance of Paul as one of the Apostles of Jesus Christ.

Acts 11:17
"It is clear that God gave those gentiles the same gift that he gave us when we believed in the Lord Jesus Christ; who was I, then, to try to stop God!" When they heard this, **they stopped their criticism and praised God**, saying, "**Then God has given to the Gentiles also the opportunity to repent and live!"**

That was the beginning, and it was Peter whom God used to break the barrier of criticism among the lambs, the sheep in the first place and the sheep in the second place for the perfection of God's children in the body of Christ. This was the manifestation of the love of God displayed by Jesus Christ on the cross.

John 15:13
"The greatest love a person can have for his friends is to give his life for them"

God first loved us and authored salvation for the sake of our redemption and we owe Him nothing except to understand His mercy upon our lives and abide by the precepts of this "love."

Before we become Christians in our standing, we were nothing at our former state and were perishing eternally, but mercy came our way and wisdom embraced and picked us out to life. It is not because we were clever enough to make a decision but that His mercy is sufficient to break the chains of bondage and bring more light as we grow up in His Kingdom! We used to start the journey ignorantly and full of mistakes in our deeds, but He is so patient to consider each of us an individual who deserves to inherit the oneness of His being as an heir of the treasure of Heaven.

The person whom God found highly lost is the one who understands the nature of the Love of God in abundance. That if it was not of His mercy upon us, we might have been dead in sin. Usually such people are the ones whose faith become deeply rooted and are the ones who stand unshakably in the Lord they believe in. In their mind echoes such words as, when they remember how the Lord rescued them, they become filled up with new strength and energy to press-on until they are thoroughly used up!

They do not have a reason to shut-up their mouths. Moreover, they are compelled by the inner drive to testify how their deliverance came about. They are compelled by the presence of the Holy Spirit to give a testimony of how they were caught-up and driven into the **Zone of Mercy**.

Let me explain the following factors, which are applicable in the real sense of operation:

Firstly, the Lambs are the people who float in the **Zone of Mercy**, and this zone covers the believers and non-believers at large – meaning every human species as a creation of God.

Ezekiel 18:4
The life of every person belongs to me, the life of the parent as well as that of the child. The person who sins is the one who will die.

Secondly, the sheep in the first place are those people who also, fall within the **Zone of Mercy**. This zone covers much of the Christian community in churches worldwide and extends to whoever has repented but not yet delivered and hence not born-again because of ignorance or their sinful-nature.

John 3:5-6
"I am telling you the truth," replied Jesus. "No one can enter the kingdom of God without being born of water and the Spirit. A person is born physically of human parents, but is born spiritually of the Spirit. Do not be surprised because I tell you that you must **all** be born again."

Thirdly, the sheep in the second place refer to people who float in the **Zone of Full abundance**, in whom the Spirit of the Lord indwells. This zone covers all the anointed people whom Jesus qualified to carry their crosses and follow Him. They are delivered and born-again as in the scripture above. They have successfully passed their tests and are approved of God to can keep the covenant of holiness as the Spirit directs.

Matthew 19:28
Jesus said to them, "You can be sure that when the Son of Man sits on his glorious throne in the New Age, then **you twelve followers of mine** will also sit on thrones, to rule the twelve tribes of Israel. And **everyone** who has left houses or brothers or sisters or father or mother or children or fields for my sake, will receive a hundred times more and will be given eternal life."

Let us carefully understand these concepts that for the first place sheep, it takes the Will of God to put His Spirit temporarily upon a person to perform a specific task to glorify His Holy name. Let us take the following scripture as example to variate between the two"

Judges 11:29
Then the **spirit of the Lord** came upon Jephthah. He went through Gilead and Manasseh and returned to Mizpah in Gilead and went on to Ammon.

Jephthah was not a prophet but was just a mere man appointed the task of leading the armies of Israel to bring victory over its enemies to glorify God.

The distinction above outlines the three levels of growth in the body of Christ, and having understood them puts one in the position of being able to bear with fellow brethren in their shortcomings and assist them grow spiritually.

The extraordinary love that the Lord has for everyone on earth is the one we should understand and be able to display to every person out there as a sign of the presence of the Spirit of the Lord in us so that we may, when fully empowered, display in abundance!

Many amongst the new converts suffer a feeling of rejection when they do not get the love they anticipate to receive from the old members of the congregation. Remember some of them come from a deep- rooted hatred and has suffered bitterly through the process of rejection from their former origins. Therefore, they might consider every man they encounter, a deceiver and a betrayer. This means that their need for true love is immense. It is at this point that they can be ushered vigilantly into the ministry of Jesus and have opportunity to learn through the assistance of assigned personal counselors, who are knowledgeable in scriptures and well trained to perform such a task.

Moreover, some of them may have come to seek the Lord having encountered irreparable emotional insult in their life, while some may seek refuge and shelter for their life from a hunt-after by the kingdom of darkness. Therefore, anticipating such circumstances, a counselor has to bear in mind to consider every individual unique, and systematically minister in a discussion form the relevant initial topics.

The counselor should be cautious to understand the newly converted person and to be able to empathize with him/her in his/her tribulations. Establishing a rapport is very important to allay such anxieties that may hinder good flow of communication and prohibit getting to the core of his/her concerns.

There is importantly no tool than building an atmosphere of trust between the counselor and the counselee (*the new Convert in this case*). This promotes openness as an element of trustworthy and guarding against being judgmental and faultfinding about their previous life. The focus of the counselor must be centered on assisting the person to understand his/her present Christian lifestyle as opposed to their former lifestyle.

Too many Converts may be burdened with challenges centered on their lives, like any other person. The following strategies may be helpful in this instance, thus: if possible, a person may be assisted to prioritize his/her challenges. Be advised to prepare to resolve, or to stay with the challenge if not resolvable as it may be a long-term issue to tackle, or lastly to move away from the challenge if possible as a last resort of attempt to bring remedy for the problem at hand. Taking a right decision at a right time is almost a trouble to many people depending on the merit of the circumstance at hand; and a person should be advised to, soberly try to apply a Biblical approach. This will prevent self-condemnation at a later stage.

Man's make up is such that he suffers regret at one point in life, and unfortunately, most of the undertakings are unchangeable once put in force. The sole advice in this case is for one to allow ample time searching for the best decision to take.

The importance of the presence of the new convert in the house of the Lord cannot be overemphasized. He/she is actually a noble person to be given all the necessary respect, and for the mere reason that he/she has come and soberly decided to accept Jesus Christ as his/her Lord and Savior. He/she should be given all the love he/she deserves because if he/she is treated with love at his/her turn, then he/she will be able to treat others who may come after him/her with love at their turn. Therefore, the law of love, "love one another as I have loved you" will be fulfilled. Remember that this law displays the love of Jesus in abundance.

In conclusion

John 14:21
"Those who accept my commandments and obey them are the ones who love me. My Father will love those who love me; I too will love them and reveal myself to them."

CHAPTER 2

Faith

Psalms 106:43-44
Many times the Lord rescued His people, but they chose to rebel against Him and sank deeper into sin. Yet the Lord heard them when they cried out, and He took notice of their distress.

There is much of literature up to this far concerning this subject, of which the scope of this book will not put much emphasis on; but which as a matter of concern I have to state my account. Faith is a substance, an entity on its own that requires a person to be able to differentiate between the personal emotions one may have and itself as a subjective phenomenon opposed to the objective understanding about it.

The conglomeration of concepts probably due to inability to differentiate the applicability of emotional facets as culminated in the mind of a person, are a major cause of confusion and a trap imposed by the devil to permanently distract the person from reaching the point of true faith, and this result into pure ignorance.

To describe it from my personal perspective: I have found it to be more of a substance that exists than a mere word and therefore a subject. I liken it to a golf ball, which has a core, rubber material and a cover, which completely secures it and make the inside inaccessible from external influences. The inside of the golf ball is described to be made of rubber material, which according to me, resembles the source that generates ***power*** that has the ability to respond to the force and pressure from the golf stick. I perceive the core of the golf ball to be like the fuel, which resembles faith, which serves as energy meant to turn the impossibilities into possibilities and the none-existents into existence.

Words run so short of meaning concerning the reality behind the concept *'Faith.'* In the true sense of matters, no one under the sun can have the basis of understanding of this subject unless otherwise revealed to him by '*Wisdom*' from above. The basis of understanding this rests on the fact of the true conception between the individual and the Holy Spirit to open up the spiritual connection and establish a personal relationship with the Lord.

Faith is a substance with life within because it can live and or die. It lives when the inner-man (spirit) is alive. Just like the physical body, it needs nurturing with the word of God to be healthy. However, it becomes sick when it is abandoned and not cared for, and the degree of sickness varies according to type of disease in progress. Amongst all the precious assets man can have in life there is none more than faith. The healthier the spirit-man the more connected he becomes with God. Amongst all the precious assets man can have in life there is none more than faith.

Hebrew 11:6
No one can please God without faith, for whoever comes to God must have faith that God exists and rewards those who seek Him.

The same concept can be compared to a man who prepares his land for the ploughing of the crops. Thus, he will need the land and the relevant work force including machinery, which is necessary to plough the soil, prepare it and make it ready to cater for the seed.

This is exactly what is taking place in the life of a person who is just newly converted from his previous life of not knowing God and his rebellious state of not accepting Christ as his Lord and personal Savior.

The reason I found faith to be more of a subject matter than an object is its credential of existence that I managed to have understanding on, through the Grace of God. I was personally subjected to stand in the gap of intersession in many instances; praying for different occasions, circumstances and conditions locally, worldwide and beyond.

It is usual that when God want to subject one on training of some sort one becomes exposed to the situation of relevancy. The reason being to, fully and personally, become involved, in order to learn and be able to help others who might not be anointed on specific field of operation.

Two facets are applicable in this instance, thus: the exposure to learning may be direct or indirect. Direct in the sense that a person may find him/herself in the situation that affect him/her personally, and requires his/her physical effort to fiddle with. Indirectly in the sense that one may be involved in a situation where he/she serves as rescuer who try to rid out somebody off his/her burdens. Irrespective of the facet, the understanding remains – that after a specified period learning should have taken place to the limit that God determined.

It sometimes happens that out of such lessons, which we are subjected in experientially, only a bit of information is revealed - meaning that a situation may repeat itself and involve one person repeatedly for learning on part of the person who must receive such until its mission is accomplished. For instance:

Genesis 37:5-8
One night Joseph had a dream, and when he told his brothers about it, they hated him even more. He said, "listen to the dream I had. We were all in the field tying up sheaves of wheat, when my sheaf got up and stood up straight. Yours formed a circle round mine and bowed down to it." Do you think you are going to be a king and rule over us?" his brothers

asked. So they hated him even more because of his dreams and because of what he said about them.

For the passage above, all key players never had the understanding of what was going to happen in the future, but the brothers were getting more annoyed every spell of time. You go through the story of Joseph in the following chapters of the book of Genesis – you begin to understand how slowly and painfully the young man, Joseph, learnt it before his full package of responsibilities is revealed to him. Could he have known the intensions of God about him, he might have developed pride that could make God change His mind about appointing him to pioneer the mission of heading his father and brothers to refuge at Egypt and save them from starvation during the period of severe famine.

However, he learnt his lessons experientially; and was humbled all the way by being subjected to physical and emotional humiliation. Moreover, throughout his story we happen to understand more of perseverance he endured, which manifested in his sufferings.

Truly, some people become exposed to circumstances that are extraordinarily out of imagination to such an extent that other people regard them sinners - who are undergoing punishment. Nevertheless, forgetting that even though they may seem abandoned for a while, they are in the classroom of their life and soon they come out of their learning situation they will be learned enough to do great exploits.

It may sound very unusual to mention the words such as 'being put in the classroom,' but the truth behind is beyond proof. When God subjects one to a learning situation – it may take an effort for one to understand and become used to what is happening in reality. Some people may endure a battery of test, which seems endless as long as the learner does not assimilate the learning content as expected. By the way, learning does not end until the learner masters the learnt content.

Psalms 32:8
The Lord says, "I will teach you the way you should go, I will instruct you and advise you."

Lack of understanding about this undertaking is a major concern for the downfall of many because by the time one is subjected to such training, one finds oneself in a situation extremely unbearable.

I have cited the example of Joseph above to try to show the length of his journey towards being fully established in the Will of God. As a human being like anybody else, he found himself a cast-out with an extreme degree of rejection, but was unfortunately helpless to defend for himself.

We may not overlook the fact that he was praying, and I believe his prayers were such that they were so touching to the one listening from the other side. Maybe he prayed to be redeemed off his hardship – but his prayers ended up unanswered the way he wanted until the Will of God is done upon him. In terms of prayers to be answered, the Will of God is a priority – this is prerequisite number one that we almost every time overlook and develop anger to Him due to not receiving the answer at due times. Moreover, it is not the will of God to subject us to any form of suffering, but suffering of some sort is a transport towards accomplishing His Will for us to grow in some instances.

Jeremiah 46:28 (NIV)
"... I will discipline you but only with justice, I will not let you go entirely unpunished."

The Will of God applies to the children of God and extends to the none-believers. The coverage for the non-believers is to see the redeeming hand of the Lord and repent from their state of disbelief and be saved. However, the span of coverage for the non-believers is limited, because they are not allowed to enjoy fully as the heirs of the inheritance of God.
The concept, 'The Will of God,' need to be thoroughly understood as compared to the 'statement of faith' and Faith as a basis of operation towards fulfillment of prayers. In short, 'the Will of God' serves as a driveway and a key to unlock the 'door of promises.' The 'statement of faith' is an uttering which serves to display the desires or intentions which overwhelms the individual concerned at a given time. What can be uttered as statement of faith can come to happen if and only if it is within the 'Will of God,' but may not happen, if it only carries the 'will of man'

which mostly caters for the charitable concerns of human sphere.' The statement of faith cannot divert the 'Will of God' away from its purpose to serve the human intentions. It is at this point, where confusion and frustration arises – especially when prayers of saints uttered in faith could not be answered as supposedly expected. For instance, if it happens that a sick person is being prayed-for for a miraculous healing – and healing does not occur.

Since we lack sight on the side of understanding the will of God with our situations, we need not lose hope but handle the concerns like Job during his time of testing. Trusting persistently without pause in the redeeming power of our God is a remedy that brings hope until the storms become all over.

Isaiah 55:8-9
For my thoughts are not your thoughts, neither are your ways my ways, saith the Lord. For as the Heavens are higher than the earth, so are my ways higher than your ways, and my thoughts than your thoughts

Failing to submit oneself under this gruesome state of testing results in a possible downfall, whereby one may regard God as being powerless to provide help in times of need, or having been ignorant to one's prayers. The fact of being a believer in Christ is a sole reason for a test of faith. Therefore behold, surely at one point in time, your faith shall be put to test. This is done to conjure promotion from one level of faith to the next in salvation.

Romans 1:17 (KJV)
For therein is the righteousness of God revealed from faith to faith: as it is written, The just shall live by faith

In conclusion

Matthew 26:42
... "My Father, if this cup of suffering cannot be taken away unless I drink it, your Will be done."

CHAPTER 3

Ascent through Trials

Teaching a new convert about the truths in the journey of 'Faith' generates a realm of justice and prepares a new Christian for the coming situations ahead. As our gospel teaches – the life in Christianity is a way that we walk through. It is like road made and well featured with the directional signs along, to give direction to the one traveling to the destination hoped for. What does this mean? It means a 'walk of life' from a familiar zone to the unknown one - a positive movement from point 'A' to point 'B' of the journey.

Therefore acting vigilantly in our stance of education to this effect turns to be a value adding phenomenon to such a person in order to nurture his growth purely without doubt of continuing and holding fast what he has in Christ.

It is inappropriate and unscriptural to tell only the good side of the story and forget or ignore to picture out the bitter side of it. New Christians ought to be taught about the exactness of growth and maturity in the Kingdom of Light. That, there are tests and trials one has to pass through from every level of faith to the next level. It is common at this point, for teachers to tell only the good but ignore to emphasize the battery of tests that a Christian life is blessed with. This undertaking is regarded a 'formulated injustice' because of giving false hopes to the person who does not know anything. The application is we have to tell the 'truth' irrespective of the circumstances. By so doing, we prepare the person to stand firmly in faith for upcoming trials some time in life.

The Love that Jesus Christ displayed on the cross is truly unconditional and abundant, but the essence of understanding is that, even though this love remains unconditional there are truly conditions that serve as the building blocks to enhance achievement and fulfillment upon a person, by Grace, underpinning the meaning of this "Love in abundance."

In the book of Matthew chapter four, the Bible displays clearly that even Jesus Christ the Author of our Salvation became subjected to some tests of faith – and that is the reason He managed the entire tests subsequent in His ministry. You peruse the books about His ministry in the Bible, you begin to realize that He went through great opposition from Satan manifested in human forms in many different occasions throughout until the time of His crucifixion. At one point He uttered:

Luke 22:28 (NIV – Encyclopedia Edition)
You are those who have stood by me in my trials

I truly need to emphasize this to you dear reader, that, sometime in life your faith shall be tested. Such tests range at the span of growth and are meant for promotion from growth to growth and from glory to glory. Just take note that every trial in its merit equals the level of the candidate to endure.

James 1:2 – 4 (KJV)
My brethren, count it all joy when ye fall into diverse temptation; knowing this, that the trying of your faith worketh patience. But let patience have her perfect work, that ye may be perfect and entire, wanting nothing.

The observation is that trials are featured according to the type of anointing the person is carrying, and works perfectly to give personal lessons to the one chosen. The connotation here is that one learns more accurately when one is exposed experientially in a situation; meaning one can thereafter testify and counsel others on the same subject one endured, knowing exactly how it is to pass through such a situation.

Let us cite an example: for a learner to obtain a university degree, he must go through a series of evaluation, prove him/herself knowledgeable on the course of choice, and accomplish the entire requirement to be credited and finally certified with an academic merit. After such lessons throughout the course of study, one has to be hands-on to participate in the economic field in one way or the other and be experienced in order to gain expertise in his career. In other words, a training of some sort is necessary for one to be fully established.

You go through the example of the Apostles in the book of Acts; you begin to understand the type of experiential learning they were subjected to, to be fully established, in the ministry. They suffered a great opposition and never were they given an opportunity to execute it with freedom.

The Will of God was that they should suffer so that His 'Might' might be revealed in their weaknesses and persecution. It takes the Will of God for things to happen in our lives; and if it were not because of His Will, nothing would cause us any kind of harm – no matter how little it may look. So many things are hidden from our sight and notion just for the sake of preserving our humanity, and very little are sparingly revealed for us to know about them.

The Lord is doing a great lot in the battle for us. Most of such battles we do not even know anything about them – for if we could know, we may faint with terror. The enemy (Satan) is working endlessly day and night looking for ways he can destroy us, but the Lord does not give him any spell to reach us. The little that is revealed to us is just merely for the glory of the Holy name of the Lord and so that we may see His power in our lives. Truly, we may not endure the full potential in our stance for our salvation if we may happen to move on without some sort of challenges. Challenges are there to deepen our relationship with the Lord, because during times of trials, it is when we mostly realize that our might and potential is full of limitations and that we cannot go on without Him who created us.

David was anointed king over Israel at a very tender age, and it took him a remarkable period to learn, from the day he was anointed until the time of the full establishment in his kingship. He was never a king just after anointing but it took him the Grace of God to be prepared for the office. God made a plan that King Saul is troubled and David become the one to provide help to remedy his situation. While in fact, the plan was to bring David closer to governance, for him to learn much of the things at the king's palace so that he may not blunder when he was to take office.

King Saul, according to the Bible, loved David to such an extent that he requested him from his father to keep him closer so that he may play some tunes to the king during bouts of attacks. However, in no time the two companions who fell in love at first turned to be enemies because of envy that emanated from the victory that David brought over Israel. David killed Goliath, and women sang and danced over the victory, but gave David more credit over the King in their song (*1Samuel 18:7*). The song was a source of trouble between King Saul and David until the day death does part them. David never enjoyed rest during his youth age and when he was a king, because of King Saul and his son Absalom. However, all what he went through never took off his anointing as a king over Israel.

This simply means that for the children of God to fall into a trial at some stage, does not necessarily mean that they are rejected or abandoned, but that out of that period of testing God will empower them and give them credit over their victory. Even though we may not like to be tested – in true sense, testing of some sort is healthy for our Salvation that strengthens our relationship with the Lord – and makes us men and women who trust in the Lord.

Trials may serve as a way through towards the full establishment of person in the position of work. They may be a scapegoat towards one's success and the success of others because the experience one gains through the period of trials makes him have a cute approach due to a better understanding on one or more parts of a subject in life. Moreover, trials are not troubles that we should invite, but are there meant to sharpen our faith for a better course in seeking the Lord.

Trials are not attacks, but are tests that serve to broaden our insight into aspects of concern for us to the Lord. Attacks are something else, meant to destroy and ruin us of all the joy we received in Christ, and are usually fabricated by Satan and his kingdom. A distinct difference is observed by making use of the following measures: before attacks come your way, the Holy Spirit will alert you and make you aware of the imminent attack in the near future – it is your responsibility to follow the alert and seek from the Lord, your responsibility during the attack.

In most of the attacks, we need not bother to do anything as a means of defence unless otherwise directed to do so by the Holy Spirit, because the alert may just be an alarm to let you know of what is happening at background. Nevertheless, God Himself becomes the one who deals completely with that attack.

2Cronicles 20:15
... The battle depends on God, not on you

Few of such are revealed to our notion and most of them are hidden to preserve our humanity. If we may happen to know what kinds of attacks were directed our way to destroy us, we may faint with terror. However, God blocks them away without our knowledge of them, but those that are revealed to us, are meant to glorify the Holy name of the Lord.

Trials are tests as indicated earlier, and can be differentiated from the attacks by nature of their occurrence. Usually, with regard to tests, no prior notion or alert will be done. They just happen at a blink of an eye and may last for a while, as God prefers you to endure. Their frequency of occurrence is more than attacks may do. For an example: one may receive a test of faith by being subjected to some physical ailment or a family member being subjected to a deadly disease.

Tests that pertain to faith are more intense to such an extent that they may be confused as attacks. This is because faith is a foundation to provision of breakthrough, but other tests that pertain to physical health of the spirit are less intense than those of faith are and may come up more frequently than never.

For an example: en-route to your destination as a driver, you come across another driver who is very reckless on the way and forcing other cars dead-break in the middle of the road in trying to avoid fatal accidents. This example shows test for emotions that those affected must distinctly pass. One distinct feature of tests is that they are abrupt in nature and usually more on emotions. One's ability to isolate a test from an attack can credit one for promptness and accuracy in treatment. For every trial, the Lord expects you to come up victorious without losing any point.

Many of the people are subjected to trials that pertain their calling if a trial is not of a classical reaping nature. For an example: a person with a gift of healings may get extensively sick so that he/she may learn to intercede for his/her cure. The experience gained out of this is a personal lesson to taste suffering in that span so that he/she may understand fully when a person suffers due to illness. This is the reason Christ is able to intercede fervently to the Father – because He personally knows, what suffering is!

Galatians 4:4-5
But when the right time finally came, God sent His own Son. He came as a son of a human mother and lived under the Jewish Law to redeem those who were under the Law so that we might become God's sons and daughters

Contrary from the above explanation reaping may come out, say, because of the offences one has committed earlier. Let me explain a little about reaping: Reaping is actually a punishment one endures, and it is a result of sins one has committed. It comes secondary to confession and forgiveness process as a vengeance that the Lord imposes over a sinner. We come across this type of undergoing in the life of King David after killing Uriah (*2 Samuel 11:15*) and taken his wife, Bathsheba, as his wife. The Lord sent the prophet, Nathan (*2 Samuel 12: 1*), to the King to expose what he did that the Lord condemns. King David confessed his sin and repented of it (*2 Samuel 12: 13*), and he was forgiven because the Lord saw the shame of his heart, but three things happened that the prophet passed over as judgment upon the King:

1. 2 Samuel 12:11
"I swear to you that I will cause someone from your own family to bring trouble on you. You will see it when I take your wives from you and give them to another man; and he will have intercourse with them in broad daylight. You sinned in secrete, but I will make this happen in broad daylight for all Israel to see."

The word of the Lord is the truth. Absalom the son of David became a tool that was used to fulfill Nathan's prophesy over King David, and there was no way out for Absalom but to do as the Lord have commanded (*2 Samuel 15*).

2. 2 Samuel 12:14
"But because you have shown such contempt for the Lord in doing this, your child will die."

In 2 Samuel 12:16 – 23, the Bible records the child born to David by Bathsheba to have fallen sick and died as the Prophet declared.

3. 2 Samuel 12: 10
"Now in every generation some of your descendents will die a violent death because you have disobeyed me and have taken Uriah's wife."

To cover up for this scripture I cite the scriptures about the death of Amnon (*2 Samuel 13:29*) first and Absalom (*2 Samuel 18:14 – 15*) last in the same generation. Please study through the book of 'Kings' and see how it all went for the descendents of David pertaining to the above prophesy.

Therefore reaping is a subject of disobedience that comes to effect even if repentance has taken place as a matter of completeness. This may be interpreted as a sort of payment for the debts (sins) done.

In conclusion

1 Corinthians 10:13
Every test that you have experienced is the kind that normally comes to people. But God keeps His promise, and He will not allow you to be tested beyond your power to remain firm; at the time you are put to the test, He will give you the strength to endure it, and so provide you with the way out.

CHAPTER 4

The Winner

John 16:33 (KJV)
These things I have spoken unto you, that in me ye might have peace. In the world ye shall have tribulation; but be of good cheer; I have overcome the world.

In this chapter, I would like us to put more focus on the successful way-out of all the challenges imposed on us by the enemy, without bringing shame to the good record of our operation.

Christianity is a journey full of tests and challenges which are meant to uplift the individual standard of faith. Such challenges are like a ladder that is used to help individuals come out of their problematic zones to the zone of full abundance of God's glory. To be honest with you dear reader it is extremely hectic for one to walk the road towards success, but our endurance produces a payout that benefit us forever.

Going through without losing focus is a benefit that lasts, but deviation is an enemy that leads to doom. One of the strategies the enemy is using is the dilution of the circumstance in order to cause confusion to a point of despair. The enemy pursues his efforts to a point of absolute desolation, and is apt to act so quick to such an extent that by the time one thinks of recovery, his intentions are tardy and the enemy becomes a winner in an instance. Therefore, applying vigilance as the Bible proposes *(1Peter 5:8)* is a best tool to go-through victoriously. Let us put focus on the following four strategies you can apply versus the three absolute strategies of the devil to win the battle. The example is depicted from the following scripture. Please read through carefully and begin to enjoy as you do!

2 Samuel 16:5-14
When King David arrived at Bahurim, one of Saul's relatives, Shimei son of Gera, came out to meet him, cursing him as he came. Shimei started throwing stones at David and his officials, even though David was surrounded by his men and his bodyguard. Shimei cursed him and said, "Get out! Get out! Murderer! Criminal! You took Saul's kingdom, and now the Lord is punishing you for murdering so many of Saul's family. The Lord has given the kingdom to your son Absalom, and you are ruined, you murderer.

Abishai, whose mother was Zeruiah, said to the king, "Your Majesty, why do you let this dog curse you? Let me go over there and cut off his head!" "This is none of your business," the king said to Abishai and his brother Joab. "If he curses me because the Lord has told him to, who has the right to ask why he does it?" and David said to Abishai and to all his officials, "My own son is trying to kill me; so why should you be surprised at this Benjaminite? The Lord told him to curse; so leave him alone and let him do it. Perhaps the Lord will notice my misery and give me some blessings to take the place of this curse."

So David and his men continued along the road. Shimei kept up with them, walking on the hillside; he was cursing and throwing stones and earth at them as he went. The king and all his men were worn out when they reached the Jordan, and there they rested.

From this extract of the scripture, let us outline the strategies that the devil tries to use in his attacks.

The devil's focus is more on the children of God. Every day and night, his business is on devising means to destroy them. It is not everybody that the devil is after, but he becomes annoyed to lose membership of one affiliate. That is why the campaigns all over the world to recruit supporters and followers. Not everybody who claims to be the child of God is truly the child of God, but there are those whom by virtue are written about in the book of *Matthew 7:21.*

It is only by arriving at a certain point of your perseverance in salvation (David arrived at Bahurim in his journey) that you are declared the child of God. It is at this arrival at a point whereby you are regarded dangerous to the kingdom of darkness – hence being sought after by the devil to make you lose focus and turn you into an ordinary man in the world, who can just have faith and belief. However, if you are an ordinary believer, the devil does not consider you dangerous to his kingdom because in one way or the other you are his fan – because of shallowness of your faith in Christ Jesus. The people after whom, the devil seeks most, are those who have crossed over from the level of mere servants and have achieved the status of being the sons and daughters of God. This is the most perilous category that Satan fears the most, and is subjected to multiple attacks and challenges imposed over them. The Lord pays no more worry on their account because He knows they overcame since creation.

There are only three strategies the devil uses to battle and nothing more:

- **Strategy number one - Cursing**

2 Samuel 16:5
..., Shimei son of Gera came out to meet him, cursing him as he came.

This is one strategy that the devil likes most and is usually the first line attempt in the chronology of attacks he may try to impose over someone. This is a profane fabricated to afflict the targeted individual in order to annoy and pursue him to commit sin in retaliation to the source of annoyance and become demon possessed through the spirit of anger. He is sure that if he curses over an individual, that individual may lose temper and begin to behave inappropriately. Remember Satan knows the makeup of man thoroughly – that is why he may have good suggestions and plans to bring about the destruction over his victims.

- **Strategy number two - Pelting**

2 Samuel 16:6
Shimei started throwing stones at David and his officials, even though David was surrounded by his men and his bodyguard.

When the devil begin to throw stones, know that he tried the first strategy and was defeated. At this point, his rage is at a better degree than never. This is when his troops are strengthened more than ever, and the battle is more intense. The intensity of the battle escalates day by day. His intelligent wing never rest, but is continuously strategizing the downfall of their victim. The focus is upon looking for the loopholes to invade the territory and seize their enemy. If they found one loophole, no matter how little it may look. They built up a stronghold from which they will strike.

Stones are such things as pestilence (of viral origin probably), any kind of infirmity, familial disorganizations, indebt and bankruptcy, any form of mishap including death of a loved one – usually being an unnatural death or death following a deadly disease. This type of death applies to close familial or extra-familial kinship that are not saved, in order to hurt you where it hurts the most, so that you begin to doubt the protection the Lord has given you. A person who is not saved is usually hard of falling within the span of coverage by the blood of Jesus and is therefore prone to demonic inflictions. Prayers can cover him, but to a certain degree, because the devil may catch him up during the time of sinning and destroy him. Such people merely swim in the 'Zone of Mercy' and are not in full abundance of God's love. Remember the story of Job in the Bible.

Job *(Job chapters 1, 2 and 3)* was going through the process of being stoned at, and believe me it was more than unbearable in his case. However, God spared him!

- **Strategy number three - Infamy**

2 Samuel 16:7 (KJV)
..., come out, come out, thou bloody man and thou man of Belial.

This strategy is the final the devil uses in most cases to try to destroy his victim. He become so sure that when he speaks bad about you or influences other people to bad name you, he may strike you at the right point to knock you down. This strategy is usually not applicable to most people unless otherwise specified. The people who are attacked using this strategy are usually very strong people who overcome every devilish attempt in the name of Jesus. The intention behind pinpoint at you is to let people run away from you in fear of their lives. The devil may publicize a fabricated ideology, a pure lie, at the expense of your name. He usually spread his intentions targeting the small faithed people who are not mature enough to find for themselves the truth behind an allegation in the spirit.

Under normal circumstances, one's dignity is a priority to one. The preservation of human dignity is a tough task to perform for an individual self. Therefore, it becomes a heartbreaking issue to pick up from the ground one's spilt image.

From the scripture above, we learn how David was insulted by the devil using Shimei's body, mind and energy. In other words, the scripture outline that Shimei's body was a transport that served the intentions of Satan. By the look of an eye, it was Shimei in his carnal body, but in true sense, it was Satan himself in hunt for David's fellowship.

When this moment comes, it fulfills the scriptures about the fate of the Disciples of Christ that:

Mark 13:13
Everyone will hate you because of me. But whoever holds out to the end will be saved

The devil does not shame to pronounce you his disciple in front of the multitude – this he does to campaign for himself against you before the people who know and give you respect as a famous man of God.

Matthew 10:28
Do not be afraid of those who kill the body but cannot kill the soul; rather be afraid of God, who can destroy both body and soul in hell.

When the devil called David man of Belial, he expected that as a warrior, he would rage and come out or assign a man to go and kill Shimei. Meaning this was a proposal for a blood treaty. Could David have acted with temper, he could have been demon possessed and served Satan the rest of his life.

The last kick of a dying horse – Combined tripartite Strategies

2 Samuel 16:13
... Shimei kept up with them, walking on the hillside; he was cursing and throwing stones and earth at them as he went.

After going through successfully and victoriously from the three attacking strategies of the devil, you may now come across the final zone where he is about to give-up. However, before he does so, he intensifies his efforts and embarks on a last attack.
The dying horse kicks the air like nobody's business. Consider the scripture above – all the three strategies were combined at once. That if the curse or the earth (sand) is a miss the stone is a hit, and one amongst the three weapons must strike you down.

In essence, there is coverage of the enemy's supporters spying over you all the way – and some playing disguise from within your camp, especially the weakest counterpart in order to bribe and device means to weaken you down. Abishai is an example of people who innocently played a protective part because of the king, but who in true sense was used to come with proposals to the King and suggest actions that will force him treaty with the devil. This is very important, Abishai was carnal and wanted to apply his strength and might to solve a problem, which in essence was spiritual. It was spiritual because there would have never been a problem between King Saul and David if it was not because of Saul's disobedience to the Lord, that led to his rejection as king over Israel *(1 Samuel 15:23)*

The enemy can invade your territory through any possible means – this usually happens in a group of people in common accord for the service of the Lord. It only depends on the strength and vigilance of the leader of the group to discern evil soon as it ensues, and deals with it accordingly. David instead of buying Abishai's carnal proposals, which came out of anger, he disregarded and rebuked him to let Shimei continue cursing for, "if he curses me because the Lord told him to, who has the right to ask why he does it." *(2 Samuel 16:10).*

Four genuine strategies for the sons and daughters of God to win the battle against the Devil

Let me first variate between the following two statuses:

- **Son/Daughter** – is a descendant of a parent. Their relationship is blood. The son/daughter is the heir of the parent's inheritance and has full rights equal to the owner over the property

Galatians 3:26
It is through faith that all of you are God's children in union with Christ Jesus.

Galatians 4:6-7
To show that you are His sons and daughters, God sent the Spirit of His Son into our hearts, the Spirit who cries out, "Father, my Father." So then, you are no longer a slave but a son or daughter.

- **Servant** – according to 'The South African Oxford Dictionary, 2nd edition' is a person whose job is to work or serve in someone else's house'. Meaning the presence of the worker in the house is to perform his/her duties and that is all. By serving and living in the house with the owner does not credit him/her the heir of the inheritance of the owner, because he/she is just a servant who is being remunerated for the services he offered. The servant differs from the slave only in the sense that the servant receives his/her pay, while the slave is being owned and works without receiving his/her pay.

All the three categories, the son/daughter, the servant and the slave may be found on the same grounds but differ in relationship to each other and the owner.

Therefore, the sons and daughters differ in relationship to the servants. This means that when coming to the battlefield sons and daughters will definitely win over the enemy, while the servants may win or lose over the enemy. The son/daughter knows everything of the Father, and the servant knows just a portion about the Father.

The Holy Spirit is the only qualifier who has the ability to make us feature in the kinship of Jesus, since He can freely offer the gift of faith *(1Corinthians 12:9).* When faith is in full abundance then the blood of Jesus has the ability to take charge. However, without the gift of faith there is absolutely no relationship. Take care that general faith does not apply in this instance, but only the Gift of Faith. General faith *(James 2:19)* applies even to the demons – and demons cannot be the heirs of the Kingdom of God. Only those who are born of the Holy Spirit are called the children of God *(1John 3:10)* – and these are the ones regarded the heirs of the Kingdom of God because of the rebirth occurred upon their lives. They are the born-again *(John 3:5-7).*

King David was a servant that is why he could not defeat sin even though he knew of it *(2Samuel 11:14-27).* Could he have been born through the Spirit in Christ (1John 3:9-10); he could have qualified a son of God. However, because of his birth date, he remained a servant until his death. Nonetheless, he and the others of his times were made to qualify through God's mercy – and were therefore not in full abundance of God's love. Those who are born of Christ are baptized in the Spirit. They therefore, qualify to be called the sons and daughters of the Lord by the blood of Jesus – they are therefore, undefeated.

1John 5:4
Because every child of God is able to defeat the world, and we win the victory over the world by means of our faith.

- **Strategy number one – Remain silent**

2Samuel 16:10
"This is none of your business," the king said to Abishai and his brother Joab. "If he curses me because the Lord told him to, who has the right to ask why he does it?"

Satan usually lays an attack and waits to see and listen to your response. From your response and or confession, that is when he knows and measures the intensity of his blows. It sounds insane to remain silent after you are blown, but it is crucial to keep quiet as if nothing happened. Silence does not necessarily mean being without words to utter, but that instead of crying and complaining about your situation, rather praise the Lord. This will keep you up above the situation and prepares you for the next turn. Satan does not have the ability to know your intentions, until such time you begin to speak out or does something. It is then he tries to hijack your thought and your actions through demonic influences. If he cannot predict your intentions, he may send someone, usually a fellow to come, discuss your concerns with, so that he knows your plans, and try a follow-up blow. However, he becomes so frustrated if you are silent. Many believers, even the sons and daughters of God lose the battle at this point. What do you think Jesus Christ' silence was all about all the way to the cross!

Why did Job never utter any word negative about His God? He never did it even after his wife's proposal *(Job 2:9)*

- **Strategy number two – Ignore him**

2Samuel 16:11
And David said to Abishai and to all his officials, "My own son is trying to kill me; so why should you be surprised at this

Benjaminite? The lord told him to curse; so leave him alone and let him do it.

Ignorance is a strategy amongst them, which is extremely powerful to knock and frustrates the opponent to a point of despair. Ignorance does not mean there is nothing happening. It does not mean that you are shielded from receiving the blows nor experiences, but it means that if you know the battle you are in, you will definitely strive for a victory. No matter how hard you may be hit – the Lord is waiting to see the day you are crowned the winner. Some blows will seek for your attention and make you lose focus, but even if it is like that go on. Wait and listen to the Lord for what you have to do next, and pursue praising Him who art in Heaven.

- **Strategy number three – Continue Along the road**

2Samuel 16:13
So David and his men continued along the road. Shimei kept up with them, walking on the hillside; he was cursing and throwing stones and earth at them as he went.

In most cases, the circumstances play around time in order to prohibit one to move forth. This procrastination (a curse) serves as a delaying tactic until time is over so that doubt ensues. Satan knows very well that time is a crucial aspect in the realm of the spirit; therefore, he may impose delay for you to be against time. The importance of pursuing along your journey cannot be over-emphasized.

People differ in perceptions anyway:

2Samuel 15:30 (NIV)
But David continued up the Mount of Olives, weeping as he went; his head was covered and he was barefoot. All the people with him covered their heads too and were weeping as they went up.

The extract of the scripture above cite a clear example of what the king did while he was in greatest despair. Many people sit down to pend subsidence of the trial at hand before they could continue with their journey. Others roll over the ground when they cry. The fact is crying or not – as long as you have not reached your destination, know that the journey is still waiting ahead of you. If you sit down when you cry, you have not arrived at your destination yet – meaning you are not safe on the road up until you arrive at the destination.

King David knew the strategy very well that for him to be completely safe is to run for his life until he reached the place of safety. He never sits or rolls over the ground in tears but he continued weeping as he went up the hill. His tears did not make the journey short nor make the uphill smooth for him – but he continued in tears and sackcloths.

Amazingly, David was known to be a poet and a worshiper but we discover him using different strategies in this case. This shows that it is not a formula before the eyes of the Lord to make use of known or somewhat prescribed method of approach in dealing with cases, but as cases are different, the approach also differs – and the best tool in the battle is to pend the order of the commander. You do not do what you please in spiritual battle, but you listen to the Holy Spirit for the next action.

Being at this zone of the journey is all about life or death. Your opponent embarks on a combined tripartite strategy to sweep you off its sight and win you over forever – to destroy you.

This is the most difficult period of the battle in the spirit. Losers lose the battle at this point, and the winners shine over after this period. However, behold the Lord trust that no matter how heavy it may be you will come up victorious. Be careful not to take an alternative road, it may be dangerous to do it that way. Just go on the way of the Lord. Go on!

- **Strategy number four – arrive and rest**

2Samuel 16:14
The King and all his men were worn out when they reached the Jordan, and there they rested

This is the point where like a racer you may utter the words of the Great Apostle Paul in the letter to Timothy:

2Timothy 4:7-8 (KJV)
I have fought a good fight, I have finished my course, I have kept the faith: henceforth there is laid up for me a crown of righteousness, which the Lord, the righteous judge, shall give me at that day: and not to me only, but unto all them that love His appearing.

Glory is for those who deserve it. After a long period of struggle, the winner becomes rewarded with the crown of honor as a sign of appreciation and reward. It is usually not an easy road to travel successfully towards success, but it is very hectic and cumbersome. Let us analyze the situation King David was in: from the city, death was imminent for him by Absalom and his companions; along the road on the other side Shimei was up against him with curses and stones, and ahead of him was a hill to climb running for his life to the place of safety. All this things were up against him and his men to do even though the time and chances were very slim to survive. The gist of the matter is that he had to keep time and do everything within a specified period.

Time is very important in the spiritual warfare. Most warriors fail their assignments due to delay of some sort or acting before time ripens in their undertakings. You cannot initiate a fight before the Captain commands you to do so, but you have to pend his order to initiate a move. This is very important a tip that many Christians use to overlook due to ignorance and fear of unknown. One other failure emanates from lack of distinction of understanding between application of faith and the Will of God at a given time. Acting against the will of God will never benefit you in anyway. Today we see people coming for a prayer and being laid hands upon for the same problem repeatedly in hope to provide cure and relief from their burdens – but without success. This means that there should be a point to closely, look-at in trying to get correct remedy for situations being prayed-for. God never fails, but servants who fail to heed their Master's voice do fail. Sons and daughters know the voice of their Father and always do according to His Will. Surely, a son or daughter will never pray against the Will of his/her Father irrespective of emotions or charitable sphere at hand. Remember Jesus when in Gethsemane, His will was for a cup of suffering to be removed but knowing His Father's Will made Him pray according to what must happen *(Matthew 26:39).* The fact of knowing in this case supersedes the reality at a time.

Let me cite this example: in the case where a prayer is made in petition for the life of a person who is sick to death – the idea is to plead for God's Grace to provide for help and petition for the sick person's second chance for life. Sons will know that the sickness of the sick leads to death or life in glory of God's Holy name and pray as cited above, but servants may or may not know. If they know they will pray like sons and their prayer will be answered, but if they do not know they will pray charitably and out of their ignorance they will commit sin of praying against God's Will.

Important: the devil use to take advantage in ignorance. If he discovers that, you are desperate in receiving the answer to your prayers and you do not know the Will of God about the situation, he brings about suggestions that will make you go far beyond what you must do, including doubt about the remedy that could take place. Once doubt escalates, mistakes multiply even to a point of total despair. Be careful to pass all your tests!

Finally, the King and his men arrived at the place of rest. The example of King David in the previous scriptures is a true reflection of the journey traveled by intercessors in their process of prayer. After fighting a good fight of faith, you arrive at your place of rest. Going up the hill is just as the same as praying fervently piercing through the higher places in prayer. You come across evil forces, fully armed, but you manage to go through in the name of Jesus. By the time, you receive your answer that is when the battle is over and you rest.

In most cases, a successful pass over a single test is a breakthrough that opens doors for bigger things ahead. Therefore, a rest may be just temporary in preparation for bigger responsibility in the future.

Luke 16:10 (KJV)
He that is faithful in that which is least is faithful also in much: and he that is unjust in the least is unjust also in much

After the entire struggle King David went through, there was a breakthrough to restore him back to his position as a king over Israel when his enemy (his son Absalom) died. You may wonder why most of the servants of the Lord struggled that much in most of the stories in the Bible. The reason may be, if God intents to make a celebrity out of you and an exemplar to display His Might through you He can make all what it takes to put you in a situation that He knows you will not disappoint Him but will represent His power as much as He has trust on you. Therefore, when something strange happens on you first find from the Father how it came about. He is so faithful to let you know so that you shine in praise, and as you shine, His Glory comes down.

Sometime He may boast about you and proves Satan wrong. When Satan swears by himself that all human races has alliance with him, The Lord can appoint you to show him that amongst all there are those who are sealed with the seal that will never fade; those who irrespective of life or death will never abandon their God. They are the sons and daughters who share fellowship with the Mighty King, Lord Jesus and are declared the heirs of the treasures of Heaven through the blood of Jesus. Amen!

In conclusion

Romans 14:22
Keep what you believe about this matter, then, between yourself and God. Happy are those who do not feel guilty when they do something they judge is right!

Chapter 5

Unison

Jeremiah 29: 10-13

"The Lord says, 'when Babylonia's seventy years are over, I will show my concern for you and keep my promise to bring you back home. I alone know the plans I have for you; plans to bring you prosperity and not disaster, plans to bring about the future you hope for. Then you will call to me. You will come and pray to me, and I will answer you. You will seek me and you will find me because you will seek me with all you heart.

There is always a commonality of understand between two or more people who share the same sentiments. Although there are some remarkable variations in every span of execution and interaction, the single quality outlined determines the full or partial characteristic of individuals at a given time. This refers to the magnetism created by being one even though individuals may not know each other but the seed of the Spirit in them connects and gives them a feeling of belonging and bravery to interact and start to know each other. What happens is that people who are possessed by the Holy Spirit cannot go around unnoticed, but even though they may try to hide away, the energy in them becomes so much that they will not hide for longer in their hiding attitude.

What pleases the Lord most in human beings is the attitude of obedience to the word, especially the precepts not to defile His position as God by substituting His Might with another powers. Like it is a usual practice nowadays whereby people run after power and the ability to perform miracles.

Some run after this to such an extent that they inherit demonic powers to perform miracles in order to get recognition and wealth from people who follow them.

Deuteronomy 5:7
"Worship no god but me"

Matthew 24:24
For false Messiahs and false prophets will appear; they will perform great miracles and wonders in order to deceive even God's chosen people

Ignorance to the word of God results in disability to get equipped with the spiritual gift of discernment hence deadly downfall in blink of an eye. Ignorance is no excuse.

Hosea 4:6
My people are destroyed for lack of knowledge

Ignorance is one satanic strategy to destroy the knowledge and prevent people from accessing truth, which is vital for their salvation. Preachers are overwhelmed by unfounded information, which they pervert to suit their own interests and continue teaching false lessons, which allure people but fail to lead them the real life. Demonic sprits are out there in force to bring about false revelation in their minds and by means of dreams and visions, which are fabricated to falsify the truth. However, because of the disunity between them and the Spirit of the Lord they even fail to realize that such is falsely fabricated to put them and their entire followers to doom. Their positions are a trap in their ways. Teaching the word of God without the Holy Spirit is just like digging a fountain on a rock.

The reason Jesus was born is to; permanently expunge the works of the devil and reunite the fallen men back to the Creator.

1John 3:8
...the Son of God appeared for this very reason, to destroy what the Devil has done.

God is the one who determined that redemption must be done the way it is, and if it were not because of Jesus sacrificing his life for us there would be no mention of it as we speak. Jesus died for the liberation of all those who believe in Him in truth and abound to keep their relationship lively with Him. God loved the world so much that He could not ignore and leave man prone for eternal torment by the devil.

However, He made it such that the world may not believe in the miraculous way He was conceived and born so that His testimony, as the one descended from Heaven, may not be accepted. It was God's plan that was undoubtedly fulfilled:

- That they could reject Him as the son of God
- That He becomes a threat to the priesthood and the monarchy of the time
- That Judas Iscariot took the responsibility of betraying Him
- That the army took the responsibility to execute His killing

So that we can be saved and receive eternal life through His death and resurrection.

Following all the above-mentioned reasons and the others, we cannot condone and let alone the pivotal role played by every stakeholder in the play around His judgment, punishment and brutal killing. Remember the suggestion made by Caiaphas the High Priest in:

John 11:50
Don't you realize that it is better for you to let one man die for the people, instead of having the whole nation destroyed?

Judas Iscariot in:

Mark 14:10-11
Then Judas Iscariot, one of the twelve disciples, went off to the chief priests in order to betray Jesus to them. They were pleased to hear what he had to say, and promised to give him money. So Judas started looking for a good chance to hand Jesus over to them.

Both of the above key players were under pressure of making the scriptures come true. All what they suggested was determined since the design of redemption by the Lord. They had no way-out to escape their assignments. The high priest suggested because he was in power and had the right to be listened. Judas had to be one of the disciples in order to betray Jesus at the end of his ministry with Him.

In most of the time, we happen to judge these key players otherwise, and that is because of ignorance on our part and lack of understanding of the revelation behind the scriptures.

John 17:12
While I was with them, I kept them safe by the power of your name, the name you gave me. I protected them, and not one of them was lost, **except the man who was bound to be lost** – so that the scripture might come true.

Let us examine the above scripture and learn that Judas had no option but to fulfill his assignment about Jesus. Therefore, if it was a planned thing since creation that he will betray the Lord, what sin has he committed that discredit him entrance into Heaven! This is one more impression that the Lord will never judge the way we, people do. One other aspect, which is of utmost importance, is that Judas Iscariot repented soon as he discovered his mistake, and was definitely forgiven. He regretted his sin in the way of the Lord and found himself not worthy of the grace, and therefore took his life.

The reason why Judas's ministry of betrayal had to end was to pave way for the ministry of faithfulness and trust that was displayed by the eleven left Disciples of Christ. Otherwise, there could now be two visions, which do not support each other. In addition, there would have been two groups of Disciples opposing each other. Remember, Judas was a Disciple of Christ who was as well informed as any other disciple in the team. That is why he had to die in order to banish confusion in the ministry of the apostles of Christ. He killed himself so that he carries the blame of his death and not relinquishing it to anybody else. For the mere fact that he killed himself it shows that it was not his fundamental intention to betray Jesus but was driven by power beyond his control. He was forsaken for a while for the fulfillment of the scriptures, and during that time, the devil took over and control Judas span of thinking.

John 13:26-27
Jesus answered, "I will dip some bread in the sauce and give it to him; he is the man." So he took a peace of bread, dipped it, and gave it to Judas, the son of Simon Iscariot. As soon as Judas took the bread, **Satan entered him**. Jesus said to him, "Be quick about what you are doing!"

Verse 30
Judas accepted the bread and went out at once. It was night.

All other disciples were faithful and strived to pursue the principle of holiness, but with Judas in his own standing, was a thief. Theft is a sin (Exodus 20:15) that Judas has been doing throughout the entire period of Jesus' ministry. Holiness implies purity – a prerequisite for the indwelling of the Holy Spirit to posses the body as His temple. Because of his impurity, Judas would never be possessed by the Holy Spirit at the day of the Pentecost – as He never dwells filthy environment. That is the other reason why Judas had to die.

John 12:4-6.
One of Jesus' disciples, Judas Iscariot – the one who was going to betray Him – said, "Why wasn't this perfume sold for three hundred silver coins and the money given to the poor?"

He said this not because he cared for the poor, but because he was a ***thief***. He carried the moneybag and would help himself from it.

However, despite all what transpired in the debate concerning Judas and his betrayal, *we need not expect to find Judas and the other two criminals crucified with Jesus in hell*, because all the three were forgiven and resurrected. Remember the mission of Christ is to reunite lost humanity back to God. Moreover, how Judas could be subjected to eternal doom while he was also the chosen like any other disciple in good standing? The other two criminals were so fortunate to die at time of Jesus death on the cross. Remember they endured the fate of death on the cross and their account of sins was paid whilst alive.

In the book of,

1Peter 3:18-20
For Christ died for sins once and for all, a good man on behalf of sinners, in order to lead you to God. He was put to death physically, **and in His spiritual existence He went and *preached to the imprisoned spirits. These were the spirits of those who* had not obeyed God** when He waited patiently during the days that Noah was building his boat – eight in all – were saved by the water.

The understanding is that Judas Iscariot died some few hours before the death of Christ on the cross, and his soul went to captivity and joined the other souls there who were waiting for the deliverance of Jesus. These souls were in jail and suffering the torment imposed on them by Satan and his demons; including all the souls of all those who died before Christ, even the souls of some saints like Samuel and other prophets who were not taken directly to Heaven like Elijah and Moses. The soul of Samuel and other big names in the Bible were all in captivity, under the lordship of the kingdom of darkness, and that is why the devil could easily, get reach of them. Let us check:

1Samuel 28:7-15 (KJV)
Then said Saul unto his servants, seek me a woman that hath a **familiar spirit** that I may go to her, and enquire of her. And his servants said to him, Behold, there is a woman that hath a familiar spirit at En-dor. And Saul disguised himself, and put on other raiment, and he went, and two men with him, and they came to the woman by night: and he said, I pray thee, divine **unto me by the familiar spirit**, and **bring me him up, whom I shall name unto thee.** And the woman said unto him, Behold, thou knowest what Saul has done, how he hath cut off those that *hath familiar spirits*, and the wizards, out of the land: wherefore then layest thou a snare of my life, to cause me to die? And Saul sware to her by the Lord, saying, as the Lord liveth, there shall no punishment happen to thee for this thing. Then said the woman, whom shall I bring up unto thee? And he said, **Bring me up Samuel.** And when the woman saw Samuel, she cried with a loud voice: and the woman spake to Saul, saying why hast thou deceived me? For thou art Saul. And the king said unto her, Be not afraid: for what sawest thou? And the woman said unto Saul, I saw **gods ascending out of the earth**. And he said unto her, What form is he of? And she said, an old man cometh up; and he is covered with a mantle. And Saul perceived that it was Samuel, and he stooped with his face to the ground, and bowed himself. And Samuel said to Saul, why hast thou disquieted me, to bring me up? ...

If we check closely at the above scripture, we realize that the soul of Samuel was said to be coming up from the ground, which is the place where the Bible declares Jesus Spirit went during the three days of His ministry to the souls under captivity. The body of Jesus was laid in the tomb, but His Spirit was in the mission of deliverance underground. The underground being the place, which he promised to one of the criminals on the cross:

Luke 23:42-43
And he said to Jesus, "Remember me, Jesus, when you come as King." Jesus said to him, "I promise you that ***today*** you will be in ***Paradise*** with me."

Jesus made a promise to the criminal to be in Paradise with Him the very day of their death, and it is clearly recorded that from the cross the Spirit of Jesus went for deliverance of the captives underground as the following scripture outline. Therefore, Paradise can never be a geographical place in Heaven as it has always been presumed, but a **Kingdom**. Therefore, the promise outlines the beginning of Jesus Kingdom, which began right from the cross. Check the timing of Jesus in verse *43* above, "I promise you that ***today*** you will be in Paradise with me."

Ephesians 4:8-9
As the scripture says, **"When He went up to the very heights, He took many captives with Him**; He gave gifts to people." Now, what does "He went up" mean? It means that first **He came down to the lowest depths of the earth.**

Now, the above scripture pose it vividly that many of the captives who received salvation in captivity were taken up with Jesus by the time he rose from the dead on the third day since His death on the cross. Imagine, for the souls in captivity, Jesus' appearance was a dire hope because there was no other hope left since they died in sin while alive on earth. These included the soul of Judas Iscariot who died in sin of disloyalty, betrayal and suicide. Not excluded are the souls of the two criminals crucified with Him. All of them Jesus ministered Salvation and deliverance, and if they repented, there could be no reason for them to be left behind when the Lord **took many captives with Him** (verse 8 above).

Job 26:5
The spirits of the dead tremble **in the waters** under the **earth.**

Another evidence of what has been happening in the three day-period of Jesus ministry in the spiritual realm is reflected in the physical by the resurrection of some of the saints who entered the Holy City during the day Jesus was raised. This was extremely ***powerful***: even the dead in the Lord could not pend the tremendous power that overwhelmed the universe at the given time, but came out alive to the visible. Wow Hallelujah!

Matthew 27:50-53
Jesus again gave a loud cry and breathed His last. Then the curtain hanging in the Temple was torn in two from top to bottom. The earth shook the rocks split apart; the graves broke open, and **many of God's people who had died were raised to life. They left the graves, and after Jesus rose from death, they went into the Holy City, where many people saw them.**

Two incidences affirming each other happened at the same time: first, in the city the relatives and friends of those who died in the Lord saw their dead alive again, in amazement. Secondly, the women disciples were battling between fear and joy at the graveyard when they discovered that the Lord has risen and ready to meet the other disciples at Galilee.

John 20:15 -17
"Woman, why are you crying?" Jesus asked her. "who is it that you are looking for?" She thought that she was a gardener, so she said to him, "if you took him away sir, tell me where you have put him, and I will go and get him." Jesus said unto her, "Mary!" She turned towards him and said in Hebrew, "Rabboni" (This means Teacher). "**Do not hold me.**" Jesus told her, "Because I have **not yet gone back up to the Father.** But go to my brothers and tell them that **I am returning to Him who is my Father and their Father**, my God and their God.

The Bible testifies that the mission of redemption was well accomplished, and nothing was left unattended because the Lord made it possible to reunite the lost humanity back to its origins. This is an implication of the incredible love that the Lord has as spelled out in the book of:

John 3:16
For God loved the world so much that He gave his only Son, so that everyone who believes in Him may not die but have eternal life. For **God did not send His son into the world to be its judge, but to be its Savior.**

That is why His judgment will have no biases because our works will testify against or in favor of us. Happy are those who lived during the times before His coming because they have been fortunate enough to get Salvation beyond the grave. Happy are those whose works will testify on their favor – "He will wipe away all tears from their eyes. There will be no more death, no more grief or crying or pain. The old things have disappeared." Revelation 21:4

The Lord clearly spelt it out that, for those who heard His word and believed the Father, who sent Him, already possess' eternal life and would never be subjected to judgment (*John 5: 24*)

In conclusion

Revelation 22:12
"Listen!" says Jesus. "I am coming soon! I will bring my rewards with me, to give to each one according to what he has done. I am the first and the last, the beginning and the end."

Chapter 6

Governance in Explosion

From the previous chapter we learnt the power that the Lord 'Jesus' used to deliver the spirits in captivity, and from then we begin to understand the scripture that says, 'for God loved the world so much that He gave His only Son, so that everyone who believes in Him may not die but have eternal life (John 3:16)'.

After the accomplishment of the mission of deliverance, Jesus was taken up into heaven now to perform another duty of mediating on our behalf (Hebrew 10:12) to God the Father as the Spirit Himself pleads with God for us in groans that words cannot express (Romans 8:26).

The preliminary phase of redemption was accomplished as the Lord managed to rise from the dead and took charge over the death and the grave. Meaning by His arousal He took the keys of death, delivered many from captivity, and had control over the grave (Hebrew 2: 15).

Revelation 1:18
I am the living one! I was dead, but now I am alive forever and ever. I have authority over death and the world of the dead.

The world of the dead in this case refers to the place where souls or spirits were being held captive over centuries before His coming. Remember, Jesus' body was put in a handcrafted tomb for three days, and tightly guarded for His disciples not to steal the body. Meanwhile, His Spirit went down to the world of the dead to deliver those under bondage and have authority over that world and those responsible of it then (Satan and his demons).

Hebrew 2:14b-15

...... He did this so that through his death He might destroy the Devil, who has the power over death, and in this way set free those who were slaves all their lives because of their fear of death.

When He breathed His last on the cross, He regained His heavenly nature with all the ***power*** he had before the beginning. That is the reason why the following scripture, because when God's presence is upon the earth – the earth responds with the remarkable loudness of joy:

Matthew 27:50-53
Jesus again gave a loud cry and breathed His last. Then the curtain hanging in the Temple was torn in two from top to bottom. The earth shook, the rocks split apart; the graves broke open, and **many of God's people who had died were raised to life. They left the graves, and after Jesus rose from death, they went into the Holy City, where many people saw them.**

The more or less, similar incident, happened in the Old Testament in the book of Exodus 19:16-22 when God came down to meet the people at Mount Sinai. Although it was gentler because the meeting was friendly – it was also frightening! In the case of the scripture above – it clearly denotes war right from the onset. Let us check the following verses of the above scripture:

Verse 51
Then the curtain hanging in the Temple was torn in two from top to bottom. The earth shook, the rocks split apart,

The tearing of the temple curtain depicts the division of the former from the present. Thus, now that it is finished (*John 19:30*), the former will never prevail against the present but the new Kingdom is established upon the earth. The shaking of the earth was a response to the presence of the Heavenly Being on it to reflect the power that, that being possessed, by splitting the rocks apart in fear of the one who created them. The connotation is the same – Prevalence of the Kingdom of God as extended down to the earth and even to its foundations.

Verse 52
The graves broke open, and many of God's people who had died were raised to life.

The opening of the graves means life again to those who were dead, thus, the dead could never rest in their graves when their Master enters the world of the dead in such a power. Those who died in the Lord rose up. This is a sign of Jesus' authority over death and the world of the dead.

In the book of Luke 23:44
It was about twelve o'clock when the sun stopped shining and darkness covered the whole country until three o'clock,

This miracle happened before Jesus died, meaning the sun could never pend to see the death of the Son. For three hours, there was darkness all over the country as a sign of impending closure of the old covenant and opening of the eternal covenant made of the blood of Jesus. Remember in the book of Genesis chapter one, in the beginning darkness engulfed the universe and light appeared.

Again in the book of 1Kings 19:11-12 more or less similar incident occurred:

"Go out and stand before me on top of the mountain," the Lord said to him. Then the Lord passed by and sent a furious wind that **split the hills**

and shattered the rocks – but the Lord was not in the wind. The wind stopped blowing, and then **there was an earthquake** – but the Lord was not in the earthquake. After the earthquake, **there was the fire** – but the Lord was not in the fire. And after the fire, there was a **soft whisper of a voice.**

These scriptures are cited to contemplate each other that during the death of the Son on the cross, was when He regained the natural of Himself to be able to transcend into the other world as God to set free the souls in bondage. That supernatural power which is able to shake the unshakables and split apart the rocks was a sign of victory.

John 17: 5
Father! Give me glory in your presence now, the same glory I had with you before the world was made.

Jesus Christ is the King, and He was made King even before the existence of time – before the beginning. Nothing can stand to oppose Him. He is established the ruler of the universe, and His Kingdom is eternal.

That power He possesses is being inherited by the 'born agains' who have acquired the title of becoming the 'sons and daughters' of God. These over-comers are declared by the Lord to be the Temple of the Holy Spirit.

The power they possess is similar to the one that is displayed in the scriptures above. Their faith is a God-given, and they use the power of confession to credit and discredit, to create or destroy. In their full-blown state of awareness about this favor, they are kings who rule beyond the spiritual and the physical realms. They are those who accepted Jesus Christ as their Lord and Savior and have kept the principle of holiness.

They are abounding to great challenges in life about their faith. Their faith attracts challenges equal to their positions in the way of Salvation to such that they may feel abandoned by the Lord. Moreover, despite whatever trials - they do not lose hope that one day their breakthrough will be at hand. Perfect understanding of the scriptures and good application thereof is their breakthrough. Heaven is their destination.

It is no wonder when sons and daughters go through some sort of trials, the reason behind is merely perfection:

James 1:2-4
My brothers and sisters, consider yourselves fortunate when all kinds of trials come your way, for you know that when your faith succeeds in facing such trials, the result is the ability to endure. Make sure that your endurance carries you all the way without failing, so that you may be perfect and complete, lacking nothing.

How can a man take a lead in the House of the Lord without having undergone some sort of training, in one way or the other? The Lord is the one who perfects those whom He loves. He does not theorize his learning, but, if you are the chosen amongst the rest, He will love to teach you His lessons in a practical real life situation. Many individuals love credits, but do not want to pay the price for such. Then one begins to wonder, because a person cannot climb up the throne successfully without first having gone down to learn upon his/her calling. An individual's successes in the calling are determined by the challenges and the failures he endured. The more the standard is raised, the more intense are the trials, and the most the standard is uplifted to glorify the name of the Lord.

Victory is upon those who have complete trust in the Lord. These people got their inspiration from the scriptures, and assurance of life to come from the Holy Spirit to endure the odds today and the good forever. Jesus Christ is the same Victor, yesterday, today and forever. He is the one who declared on the cross of Calvary, victory over sin and unity amongst the saints.

Therefore, no doubt, He fought the lasting battle that requires just a covenant with Himself through His blood to take force.

In conclusion

Matthew 11:12 (KJV)
And from the days of John the Baptist until now the kingdom of Heaven suffered violence, and the violent take it by force.

Chapter 7

Communication

Genesis 1:26
And God said; let us make man in our image, after our likeness: and let them have dominion over the fish of the sea, and over the fowl of the air, and over the cattle, and over all the earth, and over every creeping thing that creepeth upon the earth.

The word communication depends on the intent of use, and in this case relate to the transfer (Oxford Dictionary, 2007: 143), preferably of information between two or more parties engaging commonly. As it is known, there's a lot in literature written by many authors about this subject – but the aim of including this chapter in this book is to outline the context of communication between man and God – thus, trying to bring forth to the reader the importance of establishing an open flow of relations with the Holy Spirit.

It is but not so clear to many new-converts and some of the 'grown-ups' to understand exactly the conversation that is usually happening between man and the Holy Spirit. It is common in the church and out of church setting, that ignorance of teaching about such topics as this is overlooked. The reality is, the Holy Spirit communicates timeously and whenever He wants to whomever He chooses - but it may not be everybody who is able to *hear* Him speaking, and worse to *understand* Him. It takes some few factors making a barrier between man and God that are outlined in this respect, Biblically, as follows:

- **Sin**

Isaiah 59:2
It is because of your sins that He does not hear you. It is your sins that separate you from God when you try to worship Him.

Sin establishes a clear barrier between God and human beings. This is the number one factor, which is a clear means that demarcates between man and God. No man under the sun is immune to committing sin in one way or the other – which is why we remain imperfect and cannot prove our innocence before the Lord *(1 John 1: 8).* The very factor is the one declared to have caused a problem between Adam and his Creator. However, we should guard against staying behind with the **'active unconfessed'** sins in our life, but develop the habit of confessing *(1John 1:9)*our sins so as to remain acceptable before the Lord.

- **Ignorance**

Hosea 4:6 (NIV)
My people are destroyed from lack of knowledge. "Because you have rejected knowledge, I also reject you as my priests ..."

Becoming acquainted with the Word of God and embarking more on studying, paves a way to understanding the scriptures. Understanding serves as key to unlock the channels of communication, because it becomes much easier if learning has taken place that man can strive to pragmatize the learnt aspects. Whenever God speaks, He speaks in line with His word to fulfill His Will. Therefore, ignorance is no excuse, but ones choice away from the Lord.

- **Spiritual Inertia**

Spiritual lifelessness or stasis is a deadly condition, which emanates from the insensitivity caused by extreme involvement in occult religion. In this case the spirit sickens and eventually dies as a result, to such an extent that demonic forces overtakes and lead within the human body. This condition occurs in two distinct instances – there is **partial spiritual inertia** and **total spiritual inertia**. In partial inertia, a person's spirit can be resuscitated back to life through prayer and deliverance in the name of Jesus and in complete or total inertia there is no means of revival. This follows the situation whereby a cast-out, like in the case of an example in the Book of *Hebrews 6:4-6* is applicable. This example pertains to Satan and those whom he recruited for his stance:

Hebrews 6:4-6 (NIV)
It is impossible for those who have once been enlightened, who have tasted the Heavenly gift, who have shared in the Holy Spirit, who have tasted the goodness of the word of God and the powers of the coming age. **If they fall away**, to be brought back to repentance, because to their loss they are crucifying the Son of God all over again and subjecting Him to public disgrace.

We communicate to God through prayer and this is up to so far the only acceptable means of communication available; like we are taught in the book of *Matthew 6:9-13* about 'the Lord's prayer'. This prayer comprises everything that we need to present to the Lord during our prayer.

It has the following such as:

- **praise and worship**, (this can be fifteen minutes of singing or verbally adoring the Lord – *verse 9*).
- **Thanks giving** (fifteen minutes of giving thanks to every thing in our lives – *verse 10*).
- Our **requests and petitions** (fifteen minutes of speaking our requests – praying for ourselves, family, relatives, friends,

neighbors, churches, leaders all over e.g. church leaders and the governments etc, and the world etc – *verse 11 and 12*), and
- **warfare** (fifteen minutes of deliverance, renounce and declaration *verse13*).

This format can be an approach to a *one-hour* prayer displayed by Jesus at Gethsemane and it needs to be scheduled because there are times when an hour's prayer will not be feasible, this is like during emergencies.

Faith, as spelled out in chapter 2 according to *Hebrews 11: 1*, is the basis of finding our prayers heard and answered according to God's Will. Nothing will be done for us, which is not the Will of God in our lives. This statement means that there are no mishaps in the life of a child of God, but everything happens because of being permitted to happen. If it is a challenge, attack or test – God knew that it was scheduled for, on your life-map, and will definitely not destroy you, as it is meant not to – but to promote you to the next level of faith (*James1:2-4).*

Man is made up of three distinct bodies namely, the flesh, soul and spirit. God is Spirit (*John 4:24*) and whenever He communicates with man, this is done in the spirit. Even Satan does likewise in the spirit – this means that discernment (*1John 4:1*), as a gift of the Spirit is very necessary to isolate different messages and to differentiate between the speakers. Whenever this type of gift lacks, man is subjected to a trouble of being commanded and directed by evil spirits, and let astray. Which is why false prophesy today. If the spirit man is *alive* and *healthy,* it means fewer problems, but if he ails and or is dead as it is the case – it means doom.

The following are few distinct ways God can communicate with every man at a given time. God communicates to all at different times and ways; it only takes whether the recipient of the message has a healthy relationship with Him to be able to interpret what has been communicated. It takes the level of the individual spiritual-growth to be enabled to encode and interpret all messages as they are.

- **Circumstances**

This is one type of communication, which serves to forward specific messages such as lessons and teachings to individuals for a specific purpose, that man must be made perfect with God (*James 1:3*).

- **Trials**

These might range from shallow to intense degree of severity or complexity (*1Corinthians 10:13*); and no one will be consumed (*2Corithians 4: 8-9*) in either circumstance as a sign that such is permitted purposively (remember the trials of Job in *Job 1*).

- **Dreams and visions**

God may use dreams and or visions to communicate with a person of intent to deliver a message.

Numbers 12:6
And the Lord said, "Now hear what I have to say! When there are prophets among you, I reveal myself to them in visions and speak to them in dreams."

It depends on the purpose of the message and the one to whom it is directed. The variation between God inspired messages and those fabricated demonically is that, dreams and visions from God usually comes in the mornings from the beginning of the new day, and those which are demonically influenced, usually come in the evening until before midnight (NB: one must be very careful in this instance).

Contrary to the above, there are instances whereby demons mimic the way God-inspired messages are communicated; and this is outlined by distinguishing between the state of a person concerned, thus, whether a person is saved and delivered (***very important***). A person who is just saved (accepted Jesus Christ as Lord and Savior but not delivered) is highly likely to still, harbor demon spirits in his/her body. Especially the demon spirits, which gained access into a person through sexual intercourse or because of fornication (premarital coitus) and multiple sexual collaborations and other ways such as those entered through parental inheritance.

Firstly, this category of demon spirits captures the mind of a person and instills negative or horrible thought process, and influence the behavior of a person or character traits and attitudes. They also mimic prophesy – meaning people with such spirits may prophesy on behalf of the kingdom of darkness, mainly in churches. In this case, the advice is 'never listen to any prophetic uttering from a person who is not delivered,' no matter how religious he/she may seem.

Secondly, they cloud out the individual intelligence of a person and render him/her trivial and amnesic – especially with regard to academic problem solving. Thirdly, such spirits influence the sexual behavior of a person and play around his/her libido, thus, being rendered either sexually hyperactive or frigid. Their responsibilities amongst others are to destroy intimate relationships in marriages - and are a source of many reproductive diseases, congenital and different blood disorders.

- **Being in the Spirit *(Revelation 1:10)***

This is a higher order form of communication where man can be revealed visions whilst fully awake not in trance, but communing interactively in the spirit. It is not everybody who can have this type of interaction, but is meant only for those declared by God, holy. It happens out of the Will of God, and not by a human intent like in the case of astral-projection (a means of having intercourse with the spirit world by intent, usually practiced by the devil activists). It depends upon the Holy Spirit, and the moment differs in duration when that 'window' is opened for one to see whatever the Spirit wants him/her to see. In most cases it happens shortly and last for very few seconds, but depends on the criticality of the message, and hence the interpretation thereof. This is for those who are 'alert' in the spirit (… keep alert … *Ephesians 6:18).*

- **Human beings**

God can use people to deliver His messages to other people. This is the commonest way we are most familiar with – it is so common to such an extent that it attracted ignorance and taken in as nothing of importance.

Luke 6:31
But Abraham said, "If they would not listen to Moses and the prophets, they will not be convinced even if someone were to rise from death."

In as much as God can use other people to communicate His intent to us, it is clearly known that we wrestle to believe whoever declares to have been sent by God. The human element and the tendency to judge one another is our greatest point in this instance. The best example is about the whole story about Jesus – where He faced rejection and was charged with blasphemy when He declared Himself the son of God.

The message may come as a prophesy, mostly to those who cannot hear it from the Holy Spirit directly, and few factors elaborate this, thus, a person who is hard of hearing God, will himself be sent someone to deliver the message. Contrary, those who can be able to hear the message directly from the Holy Spirit, but still swim in the pool of doubt, together form part of those to whom a prophet can be sent. The distinction is that, to the latter, a word of prophesy serves as a confirmation to what is already known. This means that if a human being is completely alive in spirit, there could be no need for a prophet as an intermediary *(1Kings 22:7)* of communication between man and the Holy Spirit. Meaning a prophet is there to be a mouthpiece to those within the barrier (living in sin), but prophesy as a gift of the Holy Spirit *(1Corinthians 12:10)* is for those whose bodies are declared the 'Temple of the Holy Spirit' (remember God is holy).

Actually, the Holy Spirit communicates to everybody irrespective of whether a person is a Christian, saved or not. What differs is the ability on part of the individual, to can hear, interpret and understand the message.

In conclusion

1 Corinthians 12:7
The Spirit's presence is shown in some way in each person for the good of all.

CHAPTER 8

Fundamentals of Salvation

In this chapter, we learn about the basic requirements of salvation applicable in Christianity. The Concise Oxford Thesaurus (2007: 340), outline the following synonyms in relation to the word 'fundamental', basic, primary, vital etc. Infact every Christian as an individual and every Christian-church should possess the following golden attributes. Wherein if one or two of them miss, there could be no integrity available. These are the basics of our faith and are a reason to determine the exact growth necessary to be called the children of God; and remain heirs with Christ the Lord. These attributes are relevant to the church of today to foster the exactness and the likeness of Christ the Savior. Understanding them to the level of being able to practice them brings the church of today to the point towards the Will of God.

Revelation 1:20
This is the secrete meaning of the seven stars that you see in my right hand, and of the seven gold lamp-stands: the **seven stars** are the **angels** of the seven churches, and the **seven lamp-stands** are the seven **churches.**

They are as follows as outlined in the book of Revelation chapters 2 and 3:

- **Love (Revelation 2:4)**

The concept 'Love' in this context (KJV) is classified as a fruit of the Spirit (*Galatians 5: 22*). The Holy Spirit's presence in the life of a born-again is the one who bears 'love' as a character that indicates the presence of God in the life of a person. God is love; therefore, anyone whom God occupies as His temple possesses this attribute. It is because of this reason that the children of God are distinguished from any one else out there.

Individuals must have love, and churches must display it as an essential principle, which was given as an order that, through love, those who are the Disciples of Christ will be recognized (*John 13: 34 – 35*). This is one fundamental that need not necessarily be spoken of, but require involvement and active participation of the Holy Spirit in our lives so that we can achieve the necessary growth. Meaning without the Holy Spirit in our lives, our love is human and purely fake.

- **Faith (Revelation 2:10)**

Moreover, faith stands as a live fruit of the Spirit. The same as love, it is a very import fundamental which without it, there could be no means to please God (*Hebrew 11: 6*). It follows the same way that if it were not because of the chargeship of the Holy Spirit in our lives there would be no faith available, because all these are the results of the presence of the Spirit taking control and leading the way in our lives. It is clearly indicated that the Spirit is the one who gives faith as a gift (*1 Corinthians 12: 9*) and as a fruit (*Galatians 5: 22*).

- **Teachings (Revelation 2:14 – 15)**

The word 'teach' is defined by the Oxford dictionary (2004: 465) as to give a person knowledge or skill. Teachings in the context of this book refer to the content and or exposition that is taught, displayed, or supposed to be taught by an experienced or skilled somebody to individuals or group of people who share common sentiments. The Biblical teaching refers to a type of education, which is designed from the Bible and is contextualized to deliver the information to the Bible learners and particularly Christian believers, to give knowledge, empowerment and impart information for the purpose of spiritual growth.

It is therefore very important for the individuals, groups and churches to undergo an extensive study and research on the aspect of Christian religion so that they can be able to impart valuable information to those who follow; who might be somebody without any insight about Christianity and its contents. The importance of studying extensively is to dig as much as possible so that the type of education or training offered must be unquestionable. Moreover, because the teachings of this type, are facing some sort of resistance when they have to advance, due to some personal, cultural, religious and political influences. In essence, all Biblical teaching must be thoroughly researched and validated according to the context of the Bible itself and not be suppositional in any way or given attached meanings, which are constructed to divert the real meaning away from reality. It is imperative for all teachers to talk the same language when interpreting the scriptures. The interpretation must be according to the context of the author of the scripture, and not with added meanings that delineate the personal understanding of the interpreter.

Teachings in this context must be revelational, and this is the point where the Holy Spirit becomes involved.

John 14: 26 (KJV)
But the comforter, which is the Holy Ghost, whom the Father will send in my name, he shall teach you all things, and bring all things to your remembrance, whatsoever I have said unto you.

Without the involvement of the Spirit in the interpretation of the scriptures, there is a likelihood of 'false teachings' because our human nature and wisdom is far from comprehending God. However, the Spirit can reveal far mostly than we can do as human beings.

- **Teachers (Revelation 2:20)**

The importance of dedicated and knowledgeable teachers, who are committed to foster learning and pursue information seeking, cannot be overemphasized. Teaching the word of God is an effort, which is based on passion, which should be considered in the light of its merit and never be undermined. This fundamental requires a category of people who submit to the word and who are prayerful and eager to expand personally and spiritually in the Bible literature. It must be emphasized that the readiness of participants in this category must be such that holiness is a principle. To put it clear, teachers like any other preacher of the word of God must be free from any covenant with the devil. They should be in a position to win all their battles against the devil.

Teachers as directional tools, lead the way. They must undergo relevant preparatory sessions and be willing to develop personally as far as learning is concerned. A teacher in this case should be a person who is inclined to research and be willing to sharpen his/her research skills regarding the specific subjects of concern. It is quite important for one to discover, as early as possible in the ministry, his/her inclinations, thus, to which class of people does he/she belong in the five-fold ministries. It is very important to be well positioned in one's gift or calling, because functioning in an incorrect position of calling may cause a lot of damage to the personal self and to other people who are being serviced by an incorrectly positioned teacher. This means that discovering one's potentials and being led by the Spirit in that will spare people from a massive damage they may cause because of mispositioning. Serving in the Kingdom of God should not be regarded as a career, because careers change, but calling remains (*Jeremiah 1: 5*).

A calling is normally not an influence generated by zeal or human recruit, but it is the gift of the Spirit. Being a gift means that a gifted individual understands the contents of his calling and will be able to withstand the challenges that follow his/her type of calling. If an individual is mispositioned, this means he/she cannot survive the challenges that follow the type of duty in which he/she is appointed to participate in. Mispositioning normally comes as zeal for people to copycat their role modelers, but without being cautious about the price and prize behind. Failures in the service are usually those people who do not follow their callings, but are following what they think is their calling – this results into mispositioning and all its consequences.

- **Gifts (Revelation 3:3)**

The Apostle Paul in his letter to the church in Corinth (*1 Corinthians 12: 7)* indicated that the presence of the Holy Spirit is shown in a certain way in each person for the good of all the people. In other words, the gifts of the Spirit are under the control of the Spirit. This is a most forbidden understanding we commonly have that it takes the will of God for a gift of the Spirit to manifest. In most instances, we become blinded by a personal belief that once we performed a miracle in the name of Jesus, we can do such whenever we please. It is unfortunately not like that, but it takes the will of God and some other principles such as obedience and complete rejection of self-pride that we can be useful in the kingdom of God.

Human beings cannot use God, but the power of God is able to use human beings, thus, we need to guard against exaggerating the assignments of the Lord on us, but be able to act within the sphere of our calling. If the Lord commands, we must be able to heed His word and most importantly be alert to His way of communicating to us in different ways. We happen to miss a point today in the performance of miracles and end up taking the praise that belongs to Him. This reflects what we may have in the sin of pride, which even the devil was cast out from heaven following it!

Such gifts are mandatory in a healthy church and must be seen among the people reflecting the power of God, and not any demonically induced or magical impressions as seen in some parts of the world mimicking the Holy Spirit.

- **Authority (Revelation 3:9)**

The book of Genesis chapter 1 verse number 28 reflected it clearly that man is authorized to have dominion (KJV). Other bible translations (GNB) used the word 'control' instead of dominion, but the connotation is the same in both of them. It is upon the church of today to take control over the earth. This is a given authority to the church to subdue the earth and put everything under control. What we see happening today is a reflection of a church, which has deviated from its chargeship over the world. The church is composed of man who is vested with the responsibility to see to it that all the duties upon his span of governance are carried out as ordered.

The balance between good and bad over the world is a reflection of uncertainty displayed by man in his governance; and when the evil surpasses the good, it reflects the failures of man in governance to control the world. Then we have an ailing governor, the church, which because of ignorance is subjected to following the precepts of the world instead. The most worrying concern is the escalation of evil in the presence of the church today, which brings doubt about its governance. The today's church can be likened to a soldier well armed with all relevant weapons, but could not be able to operate a single weapon even when danger arises. This is said because a Christian church is given the most powerful weapon of them all in the entire universe, the name JESUS to use as a scepter of governance, but it finds it very difficult to rule.

Would it not be important to suspend our actions a bit, as a church, and consider a refinement of the implementation of what we supposed to do? This means trying to realign everything best so that we may admit that we lack so much of wisdom to run this government issues and go back in prayer and seek the Lord for guidance and wisdom, rather than going on blindly as if we are sure of what we are doing whereas it is evidently not.

Whom to blame, if it is the devil to blame, how did he manage to invade the church when he is not a Christian himself? The responsibility of the church is to make a good display of the Kingdom of Heaven and be able to rebuke itself where it wrongs and strive for good (*1 Corinthians 11: 31*).

- **Glory (Revelation 3:18-19)**

Isaiah 6:3
They were calling out to each other: "Holy, holy, holy! The Lord almighty is holy! His glory fills the world."

In the book of Leviticus chapter 19 verse 1, we come across a phrase that compel the children of Israel to be 'holy because I the Lord your God, am holy.' The same scripture is quoted by Peter in 1Peter 1 verse 16. In the cited scripture of Isaiah above, it becomes clear that holiness is a basis for glory that the church can possess to be able to attain this attribute. Glory reflects purity and the freedom meaning an atmosphere, which is under the control of God and a display of His presence.

This is one other fundamental, which meagers in churches today. The perception that the church has missed a point in one way or the other may sound true, and prompt a reason for research study to rule out escalating bias in the ministerial work of churches. 'His glory fills the whole world' sounds like all what He created are found everywhere and still perfect as they are. However, it is through the church that the fullness of God's glory should be revealed and the manifestation of His existence displayed.

What is wrong? One may ask! I contemplate that most of the churches are working based on perceptions and not the reality, resulting in bias of thoughts leading to negative faith (*James 1: 8*), which is sin before the eyes of the Lord. How can the church sin? Who foreruns its sinning process? The book of Revelation chapters 2 and 3 has all the answers pertaining to this question.

God never fails, and circumstances never influence Him., but His love remains constant and always magnified. His Glory fills the whole earth.

In conclusion

Isaiah 42:8
"I alone am the Lord your God. No other god may share my glory; I will not let idols share my praise

Chapter 9

The Law

Mathew 5: 17
Do not think that I have come to do away with the Law of Moses and the teachings of the prophets. I have not come to do away with them, but to make their teachings come true.

This chapter presents the information regarding the interpretation between the law of sin and the Law of the Spirit. The purpose here is to clear myths about the repealation of the Law of Moses by the advent of Christ and the introduction of lawlessness in the Kingdom of Heaven.

It is always encouraged to consider the Bible a noble treasure that should be taken into a very serious consideration. Especially when coming to make interpretations regarding the meaning of a bit more hard to understand phrases in the Bible. We undoubtedly need the Grace of God to go through; otherwise, we may become *faithful tools* to distort the truth and mislead the vulnerable who depend on the interpretations of others to grasp biblical contexts. It is merely not about intellectual capabilities but by the Grace, that we may get it very correct as the Spirit reveals that we may be vessels of honor in the house of the Lord to put it out clear without doubt to our readers' level of understanding.

The issue of the Law has become one of the troubling topics especially in the churches of the 'saved.' To start with, in agreement with the opening verse above, let us consider the following scriptures to have a clear picture of disparity between the two applicable laws that govern the universe. Moreover, Christ in the scripture above declared not to have come against the law but for the fulfillment of the proclaimed words of the prophets.

The law of the flesh (the law of sin)

Romans 7: 23
But I see a different law at work in my body – a law that fights against the law, which my mind approves of. It makes me a prisoner to the law of sin, which is at work in my body.

I perceive that anybody who encourages others to rebel against the Law of the Bible is a rebel who, by the way, cannot submit to authority, but is stubborn enough to revoke the precepts. The law of sin is declared in our natural being. It is according to Paul in the scripture above, embedded in the mind and redirects to every part of our body to impose control, which, is actually against the Law of the Spirit. These are bodily needs that are manifested as desires that no one can survive without.

The center of this law is the mind, which I refer to as a 'house of all wrongs' backed by ungodliness, and influenced by demonic spirits. Most of the examples around the law of the flesh are outlined in the book of Galatians chapter 5 verses 19 – 21, and these are all disreputable sins. The following scripture and others similar may confuse the reader to such an extent that the law referred to here may sound as if it is the Law of Moses, moreover, because it is written in capital letter in other Bible translations:

Galatians 5: 18
"If the Spirit leads you, then you are not subject to the Law."

Which law? In this case, the law of flesh as referred above, meaning the law of sin, and not the Law of the Spirit. The Bible cannot contradict itself but it is highly possible that we can misunderstand its context.

The Law of the Spirit

Romans 8: 2
For the **law of the Spirit**, which brings us life in union with Christ Jesus, has set me free from the **law of sin** and death.

Moreover, the Law of the Spirit is the one that the Lord Jesus proclaimed to have not come to get rid of, but to fulfill the scriptures. According to this law, a person has to consent and abide by it. One cannot do as one pleases but has to fulfill the requirements of the law in order to survive the stipulations. It is by this reason that Christ uttered in the book of Mathew chapter 7 verse 21 that only those who does the Will of God will enter the Kingdom of Heaven. It is stated with emphasis again in the book of John chapter 4 verse 23 – 24 that:

"… the time is coming and is already here, when by the power of God's Spirit people will worship the Father as He really is, offering Him the true worship that He wants. God is Spirit, and only by the power of His Spirit can people worship Him as He really is."

The Law of the Spirit still stands to govern the proceedings in the universe today. Since these are the last days as prophesied by Jesus in the book of Mathew chapter 24, situations are becoming worse and the pace of evil doing is escalating everywhere. The drive is too heavy to be resisted, and the naturality of the modern church has shifted to take the plight of humanism (*2 Timothy 3: 2*), but the word of the Lord shall stand to defend the truth in it.

Paul in Galatians chapter 3 emphasized 'faith' as the only thing to qualify a person free from the Law because through faith people are declared righteous by God. Faith comes by hearing and believing the word of God, to change people and make them sons and daughters of God so that the Spirit of the Lord can have a place into their hearts (*Galatians, 4: 6*). Having heard about the important message it becomes clear to our understanding that the ministry of Jesus Christ had nothing to do with the fleshly fulfillments and its desires, but the emphasis of His undertaking is based on life in Heaven. This is the reason why, after accomplishing His course on earth, he uttered out an instruction to His disciples to "go then, to all peoples everywhere and make them my disciples: baptize them in the name of the Father, the Son and the Holy Spirit, and teach them to obey everything I have commanded you. And I will be with you always, to the end of the age" (*Matthew 28: 19 – 20*).

Those who are born of the Spirit live according to the Spirit and are less likely to commit sin because they are made alert to any looming sin.

In conclusion

Revelation 22: 7
"Listen. I'm coming soon!"

Chapter 10

Deliverance – what is it?

Introduction

The purpose of this chapter is to give a brief outline of the exactness of the *Power* that the name of Jesus has in delivering people of God from their inclinations. It teaches about different problems that people have in common and brings about the remedy, and helps the ministers on how to go about assisting people who are in dire need of deliverance. This is a detailed format to prepare those anointed in the ministry of deliverance to take heed and have a point of departure in their calling. This chapter is included in this book to inform you the newly converted person to not rest but seek to be helped according to the processes of this book in order to heal you completely and be prepared to be born again, and be the Temple of the Holy Spirit.

What is it?

The word "deliverance" according to Oxford dictionary imply "to rescue". The Bible context of "deliverance" implies that it is a **component of Salvation,** which serves to rescue people of God from the imprisonment by the kingdom of darkness. It is a **means to set them free** of bondage and qualifies them to be born again; thus if a person is born again it is possible for him to be rendered holy by God. It is an outline of promises of God in the Bible to all those who fear Him.

In simpler terminology - **there is no deliverance without salvation and no salvation without deliverance.** The two concepts work interchangeably and there is no one without the other.

The greatest issue about these two concepts is that, although they are sometimes used synonymously, they are not practically one thing. However, one concept (deliverance) forms part of the other (salvation) to make it whole (perfection/holiness).

Secondly, an approach to understanding these concepts is basically spiritual – therefore without the intervention of the Holy Spirit to bring about His interpretation there would be no understanding and therefore ignorance and persistent death.

In fact, no man can deliver one another, but can only assist those who need deliverance to achieve the state of being delivered. It is only Jesus Christ the Author and the finisher of deliverance who can precisely complete the work of deliverance and set the captives free.

> Isaiah 61:1-8
> The Sovereign Lord has filled me with His Spirit. He has chosen me and sent me to bring good news to the poor; to heal the broken hearted; to **announce release to captives and freedom to those in prison.** He has sent me to proclaim that the time has come when the Lord will save His people and defeat their enemies. He has sent me to comfort all those who mourn. To give to those who mourn in Zion joy and gladness instead of grief; a song of praise instead of sorrow. They will be like trees that the Lord himself has planted. They will all **do what is right.** And God will be praised for what he has done. They will rebuild cities that have long been in ruins.

The trouble with the church today is the degree of escalating ignorance on part of deliverance, especially on how to go about assisting individuals who need it. Everybody may have an insight about how the situation should be God-wards but may have difficulty getting it right on what to do to get it right. I wrote extensively about the concept deliverance in the previous book as a highlight and a step in the process of salvation. However, with a concern that some people may be so intelligent that they attempt to practice deliverance without insight and a **relevant anointing** to do the work and therefore end-up in a very serious danger from the kingdom of opposition.

However, in this chapter, the 'Spirit of the Lord' directed me to elaborate about it to inform the world that it **is appropriate and there is no breakthrough without it.**

No matter how great a person can be considered before the eyes of the people, if he/she is not delivered – he/she is still under bondage. Moreover, if one declares that he/she is delivered but is still able to **commit sins** – he/she is still a **captive** and therefore is **not** born again; and if not born again he/she cannot not be declared holy!

1 John 3:9
None of those who are children of God continue to sin; for God's very nature is in them; and because God is their Father – they cannot continue to sin.

Deliverance entails breaking of covenants made with the devil and his kingdom, and erasure of curses that prevail in a person as well; and a proclamation of blessings upon himself plus a dedication of one's life in leading a holy life, free of sin!

Covenants upon a person can be direct or indirect. A covenant is an agreement between two or more parties for mutual concession to function harmoniously and it remain in-force as long as it is not broken; it affects everything of a person who established it. A curse is a profane over the life of an individual that remain active throughout his root until its third generation:

Exodus 20:5

> Do not bow down to any idol or worship it, because I am the Lord your God and I tolerate no rivals. I bring punishment on those who hate me and on their descendants down to the third and fourth generation.

There are two classifications of covenants outlined as indirect and direct according to the scope of this book below:

Indirect covenants

Indirect covenants are binding agreements, which an individual entered into with the kingdom of darkness. They affect the individual's life and are not established by the person himself but individuals enter into them through birth. Most of them are customary and apply to a person since conception; through the birth process until death; and remain active and binding unless otherwise broken.

Direct covenants

In this case, the agreements are established by the person himself, knowingly or unknowingly with the devil or through the agents of the kingdom of darkness such as traditional doctors, witches, false prophets etc, and through practice such as those prohibited in the Bible.

- **Knowingly** – applies to a person who is aware of the covenant and consent to it willfully or is forced to consent. It usually applies to those people who consented to serving Satan.

- **Unknowingly** – applies to a person who is unaware or ignorant on part of the covenant. This type of agreement is mostly entered into through customs and rituals of a certain group of people in a society, and is considered a way of life or religious practice to such a group.

Major types of covenants

The following are the three major types of covenants that are very binding and become so difficult to deal with especially when a person wants to quit and render them invalid in his/her life. They are spelled out in order of intensity and severity:

- **The blood covenant**

  This is one form of a covenant, which is regarded extraordinary binding because of the shedding of blood involved during its establishment; the reason being the sacredness of the blood and the life in blood itself.

  Exodus 24:8
  Then Moses took the blood in the bowls and threw it on the people. He said," This is the **blood that seals the covenant** which the Lord made with you when He gave all this commands."

  Leviticus 17:11
  The life of every living thing is in the blood; and that is why the Lord has commanded that all blood be poured out on the altar to take away the people's sins. **Blood which is life** takes away sins.

  Matthew 26:27-28 (NIV)
  Then He took the cup, gave thanks and offered it to them saying:" Drink from it all of you." This is **my blood of the covenan**t which is poured out for many for the forgiveness of sins."

We cannot over emphasize the meaning of the scriptures above, but have been included in the scope of this chapter to bring understanding to the reader about the origin of the covenant by means of blood.

Moreover, to bring you closer to the understanding that most of the good things designed by God were overturned and reshaped otherwise by the kingdom of darkness for its benefit and leading people astray of God's Will; whereby the use of human and animal blood is a priority in determining a committed covenant with Satan, and becoming his disciples. This satanic covenant is accomplished by usual ritualistic practices, which to some extend involve:

- Live transfusions (blood is shed through a cut of those undertaking a covenant)
- Accidents caused by satanic agents (resulting in bloodshed)
- Tattooing
- Acupuncture (a medical undertaking meant to relieve pain)
- Drinking of blood
- Animal slaughter purported for ritualistic practices
- Abortions (which are not for medical reasons)

Covenant through sexual encounter

This is one form of covenant, which is extremely dangerous and binding. In this case, people usually signup for this type of agreement with the devil during sexual intercourse amongst them or with animals (bestiality) either knowingly or unknowingly or by being forced to disobey the word of God or being ignorant on its part:

Exodus 20:14
Do not commit adultery.

1 Corinthians 6:18
Avoid immorality. Any other sin a man commits does not affect his body; but the man who is guilty of sexual immorality sins against his body.

Most of the people enter into this covenant at their very young age while they are still exploring love – usually at their early teens. Moreover, what happens during coitus is the exchange of demonic spirits from one partner to the other and inhabits the sexual organs of each partner and influence the mind thereof.

These demonic spirits are responsible for influencing the behavioral pattern of such an individual with regard to relations imposing lust; and are a source of many rejections and divorces at a latter life. Their presence in a person determines hatred and unforgiveness; with underlying anger and hostility which manifests during the course of that person's life.

Thus, the more sexual encounter the person has with his/her partners; is the more multiple exchange he/she has and the more demonic possessed he/she become. The state of his/her possession (by demons) influences his/her state of marriage and other relations of the same kind.

In true sense: The sins that one commits today turn to be inequities if not confessed and forgiven; and are future curses to your generation through inheritance.

Understand this clearly: if a person's life does not have active covenants established by him/her, he/she might highly, likely carry curses of the same sort as an inheritance from his parents during conception – if such parents were not delivered on this account. This is one reason why marriage partners who were both virgins become challenged also in their establishment.

The most common sin, which in one way or the other affects and entraps many - is the one through sexual intercourse. Because a demon possessed person cannot say **no** to the evil drives behind. Usually he/she does what he/she does not like; but is being superseded and forced to do it. Let us check the following scripture and see how it originated.

Genesis 6:1-2

When the human race has spread all over the world; and daughters were being born; **some of the heavenly beings saw** that these young women were beautiful, so they **took the ones they liked**.

The heavenly beings referred to above are demons; and they had sexual intercourse with human–women and bore children, which are a mixture of the two.

Genesis 6:4 (NIV)
The Nephilim were on the earth in those days, and also afterwards – when the sons of God went to the daughters of men and had children by them. They were the heroes of old; men of renown.

It is following this reason that God sent the flood to wipe off that generation that was meant to pollute the human race; but spared only Noah and some few of his household and birds and animal species. God cannot tolerate any rival.

The effects of demonic influence

The demons of sex have influence on the following:

- **The mind**

The first thing the demons, which entered through sexual intercourse attack in the human body is the mind of the person they possess. They influence the person's thinking and mould the character. The person's thoughts are mere evil; the demons will influence his/her dreams; he/she may have visions and hear voices, which usually give orders and proclaim to be "**god**." They are the type of people who serve as Satan's agent to prophesy in churches and mislead. They usually target the leadership of the church. It is very difficult to discern the spirit behind their prophetic utterings, unless the prayer graph of the church is constantly elevated.

- **The behavior**

The behavior of a person become influenced and diverted to become devilish to the extent that he/she is also not comfortable about his/her attitudes in certain situations. However, because he/she is demon possessed, there is nothing he/she can do to remedy him/herself from what he/she does not want about his/her behaviors. The most common manifestation is related to emotions such as short-temper, lust, anger and bitterness.

- **Influence on sexual organs**

People who are infested with this type of demons may display hyperactivity in sexual relations probably driven by elevated libido; or may present with frigidity. A form of deadly infections, which are transmissible through sexual contact and cancers are few common examples.

A Spoken word (confession)

This is the last dangerous form of establishing a covenant. People partake in this type of covenant due to their ignorant speeches and utterings usually by confession.

Proverbs 18:21
What you say can preserve life or destroy it; so you must accept the consequences of your words.

Some enter the covenant willfully and knowingly; and others are being forced to participate as a form of punishment or force. For an example:

- When speaking to the dead or making a mere adoration of any kind towards the dead. In fact speaking to the dead is actually establishing communication with the kingdom of darkness, which imposes certain spiritual rights over him. The dead are dead and can never participate in anyway to the living.

Ecclesiastes 9:5
Yes, the living knows they are going to die but the dead know nothing. They have no further reward; they are completely forgotten.

Ecclesiastes 9:10
Work hard at whatever you do because there will be no action; no thought; no knowledge; no wisdom in the world of the dead – and that is where you are going.

Psalm 115:17
The Lord is not praised by the dead, by any who go down to the land of silence.

It is a usual ritualistic practice in many nations of the world to pay extraordinary homage to their loved ones in times of death to an extend of turning them into gods – with the unfounded believe that they are in Heaven and will mediate on their behalf for their prayers and requests to God Almighty. This ideology has no basis at all.

Please do not be deceived. Jesus Christ will come back for the judgment of the dead and the living; and if your doctrine teaches that all the dead are in Heaven with God – then what will be the reason for Christ's coming back? For whose judgment will He be coming? Heaven is only **for** the righteous.

- Alternatively, consulting mediums in this case, the covenant is established through fortune telling by so-called prophets, witch doctors, and others of the same spirit. It is an established verbal consent with the kingdom of darkness because all the above classification and others is an agency surrounded by demonic spirits.

Deuteronomy 18:10
Don't sacrifice your children in the fires on your alters; and don't let your people practice divination or look for omens or look for spells or charms; and don't let them consult the spirits of the dead. The lord your God **hates** people who do these disgusting things; and that is why He is driving those nations out of the land as you advance.

Curses

A curse is a profane proclaimed over a person and usually determines the future of that person and his/her generation. It does not pronounce luck and good will but only doom.

Some curses are a result of disobedience to the word of God irrespective of the reasons behind such, ignorance being the main reason. (Read Exodus 20:5 to learn about generational curse and Deuteronomy 28: 15 - 68).

Some curses are due to absence of protection and security from God that leads to free flow and easy attachment of curses from every direction. A curse remains with the person as long as he/she lives, and it is transmissible down the generation. It remains active until means become available to break and root it out of the person's life. So far, there is no means available to provide treatment to such, except the name, Jesus.

Acts 4:11-12
Jesus is the one of whom the scriptures says," The stone that you builders despised turned out to be the most important of all. Salvation is to be found through Him **alone**; in **all** the world there is **no one** else whom God has given who can **save** us."

The following are examples of curses that are commonly applicable and affect people in diverse numbers; but there are those that are too specific and applicable only to isolated individuals – as cases are not the same - and become known only during deliverance counseling:

- **Poverty**

  Poverty is one type of a curse, which is applicable in most of the people; irrespective of their professional caliber and salary, they earn – but they suffer poverty in terms of expenditure and debts they have to pay from their monthly income. Most are left with nothing to save for the future.

  Deuteronomy 28:38-39
  You will sow plenty of seed but reap only a small harvest, because the locusts will eat your crops. You will plant vineyards and take care of them, but you will not gather their grapes or drink wine from them because worms will eat the vines.

  Also be careful in this instance that when a person commit sin – is subjected to reaping the fruits of the wrongs he committed. For an example: **stealing**, itself opens channels for free flow of spirit of lust (demons) into a person and is likely to steal habitually.

This subjects a person to paying the price of his/her actions – no matter how little the stolen items may look, but is apt to pay. Therefore some people suffer poverty today because of the "to steal" sin they committed.

The remedy we receive for our sins in the blood of Jesus is when we confess and repent from wrongful deeds – but **reaping the fruits of our deeds is inevitable**. Yes, forgiveness and cleansing will be done by God if one truly shames for his/her sins; but he/she still has to suffer the consequences of his actions.

2 Samuel 12:12
"You sinned in secret but I will make this happen in broad daylight for all Israel to see." "I have sinned against the Lord." David said. Nathan replied," **The lord forgives you**; you will not die. But because you have shown such contempt for the Lord in doing this – **your child will die"**

- **Death at the young age**

Too many mishaps occur amongst the people at a larger scale and affect individuals very frequently to such an extent that people become used to them and find them usual to take place – whereas they, truly, are genuine classification of curses. You may come to understand this clearly, if you are a member of a generation affected by this type of curse.

The type and the causation of death to individuals of such a generation is a marker to identify whether the classification can be a curse, demonic or just a mishap; as well as the trend and the frequency of such. For an example: some generations suffer loss of a member(s) habitually at a certain specific time of a year with the type of death being the same as of other family members who are deceased.

It only depends on the type of covenant and the degree of engagement their elders had with Satan. If they had a blood covenant – their descendants are definitely going to suffer accidental deaths; and this affects same sex as the initial bearer of the covenant first, and then to the opposite sex of the same root. People affected by this type of curse die very young and they do not grow to their full old age.

Genesis 25:8(NIV)
Then Abraham breathed his last and died at a **good old age**; an old man full of years, and he was gathered to his people.

- **Illness (Disease)**

A healthy body free of infirmities or disease is a blessing. Two classifications of conditions that are causative factors for ill health are applicable. The first one being that: a human body is a structure of tissues and organs with multi-systemic function interrelating to each other constituting a man. It happens in some stages in life that one part of the body malfunctions; and this may naturally affect all other body systems resulting in a state of illness and or disease.

Even if this state of affairs seems acceptable, it does not erase the fact that God created a perfect man free of ill health. Moreover, that death and ill health are the results of a downfall of man due to sin in the Garden of Eden. Following this statement, we may conclude that some of the words describing painful situations like death were not inclusive in the ancient dictionary.

Therefore, an ill situation is a component of a curse imposed by God. (Genesis 3:14-19) Where the remedy is:

Romans 6:22 (NIV)
But now that you have been **set free from sin** and have become slaves to God; the benefit **you reap leads to holiness and the result is eternal life.**

The second classification being that:

Romans 6:23 (NIV)
For the wages of sin is death; but the gift of God is eternal life in Christ Jesus our Lord.

Sin is the greatest portal of entry for demonic spirits responsible for inflicting and tormenting the human body and causing diseases. For an example hatred and unforgiveness results in a very serious muscle pains of unknown origin; that cannot be scientifically diagnosed by any medical means. In addition, if no diagnosis is achievable; there is absolutely no remedy within the medical field for that type of pain. Analgesics can only relieve it but can never cure it – after all pain is a symptom of an underlying condition.

Therefore, the spiritual diagnosis revolves around counseling and establishing the history of such a typical condition generationally; and the social history of the individual that may be the result of his/her anger that leads to a **sin of unforgiveness and hatred**. If either is positive; no ways the individual is demon possessed – and the treatment should be intervened spiritually.

Be careful that casting demons out of that person's life will not help if the diagnosis is improper– you will be exhausting your energy for nothing. Target the causative factor and rather counsel the person towards forgiving and forgetting; and advice him/her to advance such measures leading to curbing hatred and be forgiving. Thereafter pray for his/her healing and cast out such evil spirits. Warn him/her that his/her healing relies on his obedience to the word of God.

Do not forget to pray for his/her protection in the blood of Jesus! Monitor him/her and follow him/her up; otherwise he/she is going to die of the same condition if not properly healed, and advice him not to commit sin anymore.

NB: Please do not deprive the person an opportunity to seek medical help – this will also assist you glorify God at the relevant time. Be careful that as long as there are means, a person can do to find himself remedy God will not act.

Matthew 11:28-29
Come to me all you who are weary and burdened; and I will give you rest. Take my yoke upon you and learn from me; for I am gentle and humble in heart – and you will find rest for your souls.

- **Abuse**

Abuse is any form of ill-treatment that affects the personal being of an individual and threatens his integrity as a person. It can be physical (assault, sexual, depreciation, defamation of character etc), emotional (harassment, scorning, mocking, depriving) or spiritual (disaffiliation, spiritual bankrupsy and forced affiliation).

Anger is the foundation of every form of abuse we can spell; and it is driven by the evil spirits in a person and the demons around; influencing him convincingly to behave inappropriately. The person becomes **sure** that the decision he/she is taking is the sole application he/she must undertake to curb the prevailing predicaments of his/her life.

For an example: a sexual perpetrator is forced to rape because of the spirit of **lust** capturing his/her mind terrain. He therefore cannot refuse the drive because his instincts are under demonic control.

In fact, the person is able to realize the wrong he/she is about to commit, but he/she unfortunately cannot refute doing it. This is a sign of spiritual captivity whereby no worldly means can provide remedy.

Many people suffer abuse and become acquainted to the suffering as if it is something supposed to be; and some think that is how it should go on. There is one form of abuse, which is mostly prevalent;

and it applies between intimate people in their relationships, called silent abuse.

- **Silent abuse**

The silent abuse is a form of abuse taking place usually between lovers, and or spouses in a family or in a relationship. It is silent because it does not come up the way of abuse direct. In this case, the perpetrator is doing acts of love still harboring aggression, which manifests at certain spell in their interaction without compromising the situation. The commonest example being intra-marital rape, between married couple, or fighting over finances. Simply the driving force is the spirit of lust and of stinginess.

It is inheritable and usually manifest as anger under normal circumstances and happens to escalate to the best degree as time goes on.

In most instances, the abuser suffered abuse in one way or the other earlier in his/her childhood. Moreover, that suffering subjected him/her to demonic captivity and possession. Unless otherwise an individual becomes delivered on this part, the spirit of abuse manifested as anger will follow him/her all the way to death.

- **Vagrancy**

The person with this type of curse becomes a wanderer and has no settlement in every place he comes to stay. Because of the driving spirits in him/her, he/she always becomes dissatisfied in every surrounding he finds him/herself in. The commonest reason being unresolved quarrels with other people he/she interacts with. It does not matter to him/her what asserts he has accumulated in a specified place, but is determined to shift from one place to the other irrespective of wealth. He/she ultimately becomes homeless because of the non-fulfilled unknown innate desire. People with this type of curse usually desert their belongings and go and look for a place or job they think can curb their thirst.

Genesis 4:12
"If you try to grow crops; the soil will not produce anything. You will be **a homeless wanderer on earth."**

- **Depression**

Depression is defined as a state of mind characterized by extreme despair and hopelessness that are inappropriate and out of proportion to reality (Mosby's Dictionary of Medicine, Nursing and Health Professions, 2006, p. 537). It commonly affects women in larger numbers than men; and it is a result of unresolved conflict applicable, and follows failure to get settlement of interests. Its trend is generational because of abuse and frustration imposed over women and children by husbands or any kinship. If one parent happened to suffer any curse – it is highly likely that his/her children also suffer the same.

Deuteronomy 28:28 (NIV)
The Lord will afflict you with madness, blindness and confusion of mind.

- **Rejection**

This type of curse usually follows a person from his conception. Teenage pregnancy is a mother source of this curse because a teenager may fall pregnant or impregnate his girl friend; and this result in conflicts between their parents when trying to rich settlement of children's misbehavior.

The fact that conception occurred out of wedlock; and that the boyfriend might have feared to take the responsibility to nurture the mother and the unborn child due to his age and immaturity results in one parent rejecting the unborn child. Moreover, the offspring shall bear the consequences of conflicts and rejection as a curse therefore.

People born out of such conditions carry pre-marital pregnancy and rejections curses and are apt to suffer rejection everywhere. However, because they were rejected; they are definitely going to reject their spouse and children at a long run. This is one reason for divorce or desertions and remarriage.

- **Lust**

Lust is defined as an extreme desire (Oxford Dictionary, 2004, p. 269), in a person, which is characterized by lack of instincts to refute the drive; and perpetuates the person to 'act' in order to satisfy his desire. The person is compelled by the evil spirits to behave inappropriately. There are different types identified:

Lust for sexual gratification

Fornication – includes any sexual encounter pre-maritally.
Adultery - any extramarital affair between a married person and the other.
Sodomy – any sexual act between people of the same sex.
Masturbation – any act on oneself to get sexual gratification.
Voyeurism –– defined as a psychosexual disorder in which a person derives sexual excitement and gratification from looking at the naked bodies and genital organs; or observing the sexual acts of others – especially from a secret vantage point (Mosby's Dictionary of Medicine, Nursing and Health Professions. 2009, p. 1963).
Bestiality / zooeratia – sexual relation between a human being and an animal (Mosby's Dictionary of Medicine, Nursing and Health Professions. 2009, p. 207).

All this are compulsive behaviors driven by the evil spirits on the person they posses. The results of one's engagement in these examples are broken intimacy, marriage disorganizations and divorce.

Lust for wealth

1Timothy 6:9-10 (NIV)
People who want to get rich fall into temptation and a trap; and into many foolish and harmful desires that plunge men into ruin and destruction. For the love of money is a root of all kinds of evil. Some people eager for money; have wandered from the faith and pierced themselves with many grieves.

Be careful how you accumulate your wealth lest you become endangered. The consequence of wrongfully accumulated wealth is solely poverty. Stealing and cheating are a sole source of bankrupsy and beggary.

- **A miscarriage**

This may be a result of medical, obstetric and or gynecological condition of a woman at the time of conception or during pregnancy. Alternatively, adverse effects of certain medicament drugs no matter what the reason behind may be; the fact is it is an abnormal occurrence, which is spiritually classified under curses. Some women are habitual aborters; and the trend is generational.

In some people, this follows because of accumulated demonic spirits, which invaded them during their time of multiple partnering; especially during youthful age through coitus. These spirits are also responsible for intra-uterine deaths, malformations, mental retardations and handicap.

Revelation 12:2 and 4 (NIV)
She was pregnant and cried out in pain as she was about to give birth. His tail swept a third of the stars out of the sky and flung them to the earth. The dragon stood in front of the woman who was about to give birth; so that he might devour her child the moment it was born.

Be careful that wherever there is bloodshed; there is a likelihood of the presence of demonic spirits.

- **Gynecological Diseases**

These are the diseases affecting women and much are inheritable and include hormonal implication; while others are a result of bad sexual history of a person affected or her partner, (evil spirits play a very pivotal role here).

Mark 5:25-28
And a woman was there who had been subject to bleeding for twelve years. She has suffered a great deal under the care of many doctors and had spent all she had; yet instead of getting better she grew worse. When she heard about Jesus; she came up behind Him in the crowd and touched his cloak. Because she thought, "If I just touch His clothes I will be healed." Immediately her bleeding stopped and she felt in her body that she was freed from her suffering.

- **Childlessness (a result of infertility)**

Truly speaking, nobody knows what is happening during the developmental process of a human being and animals as well. Research can only determine some processes of human and animal development but cannot reach the core.

For an example:
The information concerning the how-abouts of the placement of each part of our bodies at its relevant place of functioning during development remains a scientific problem to conclude about. Moreover, the easiest way to attempt this concern may be that a human being is a human being and can never bear anything else.

Nevertheless, in true sense; the fact is that whatever is concealed for human intelligence, vigilance and reach is for God and is without question.

Deuteronomy 29:29
"There are some things that the Lord our God has kept secret; but He has revealed His law, and we and our descendants are to obey it forever."

It is the will of God for human species to multiply without restrictions on earth (Genesis 1:28).

Infertility is not a new problem on earth. Even during the times; in the Old Testament; we read stories of some families who suffered it and got a breakthrough through intensive prayers. We can quote the family of Abraham and Sarah in *Genesis 21* and of Elkanah and Hannah in *1 Samuel 1.*

This item is inclusive in the process of deliverance to remedy whatever situation, may follow an individual impeding multiplication of people through him/her and being a result of curse.

In some instances, Infertility comes because of witchcraft, but in rare cases. The most prevalent reason for it is the result of demon affliction on individuals.

Remember that conception under normal circumstances is following a union between male and female during coitus; and this is the field, which gained much favor in the kingdom of darkness. Thus, many people become demon possessed through sexual contact.

- **Procrastination**

Procrastination and postponement are typical curses meant to delay the progress and the fulfillment of the mission in a specified period. This type of curse is accompanied by every valid reason sensible enough to convince that there should be a delay of any kind.

Yes, there is a delay imposed by God in fulfilling the prayers of His children; but this one is meant to let the child of God receive his/her blessings at the correct relevant time, and for God to glorify His holy name then. Moreover, the one who prayed knows that his/her prayers will be answered at a specified time. Bearing in mind that a prayer is made fervently in spirit; – meaning that the answer is also in spiritual form and has to be transformed into the physical form to lay a testimony.

For an example if one requests a nice car from God, it will take the Will of God, the worldly order and the standing of a person who made a request to receive what he/she asked from God. Just imagine if you can find a nice car of your dreams in you garage in the morning when you wake up! Are you going to accept it as your car? Will you not call the police to investigate the criminal who opened your garage door and put the car inside while you were asleep and what if your salary could not afford the car maintenance!

In this case, the understanding is that, God may rather assign somebody to give you a car as a present or make it possible for you to buy that car you desired so that you are able to testify His mercy upon you. That you may not be undergoing inquests on criminal cases as to where did you get the car while, maybe, you are known not to can afford it.

However, with procrastination, the aim is to impose failure and produce lack of interest until everything good is dropped. This usually takes place where there is a breakthrough meant to remedy the person's situation and bring about a relief on his/her prevailing situation. Many people suffer this situation without insight of what is taking place in the spiritual realm concerning their prosperity.

There are a lot of covenants and curses, which apply to individuals that are not specified here, but the above is just a highlight of how to go about digging through the journey because people differ.

Counseling

Conducting deliverance counseling requires the mercy of God. It is not about wisdom and vigilance, but it is about the Holy Spirit and His gifts of uttering. It is not easy, I must tell, to dig out the hidden truths about a person pertaining his captivity and engagement within the kingdom of darkness.

Deliverance is laboring – and it requires dedication, passion and commitment. The counselor must be a trustworthy, humble sober-minded and non-gossipy person. He must have tact to initiate conversation and vigilantly be able to establish a rapport.

The environment must be such that there are no disturbances around and any form of distractions. It must be quite enough to let the Holy Spirit take control of the situation and give guidance to the counselor(s) and the counselee. The importance of the availability of time cannot be over-emphasized.

Even though the captive is still under bondage; the fact is that during counseling and any kind of meetings pertaining to deliverance – it is the Holy Spirit who controls the situation. Under normal circumstances the evil spirits harboring the person would not allow him divulge any information that pertain the kingdom of darkness.

Some individuals used to display confusion of mild degree and forgetfulness or absent-mindedness and staring; while others display a manifestation of a trance. These are signs mostly applicable; and the symptoms cover falsifying (telling lies to hide the truth) and exaggeration syndrome (pretending as if demons are exorcised). It is around this era whereby most deliverance workers become possessed themselves in the process of deliverance.

When undertaking this type of task – we warn you to be free of any active unconfessed sin, and not to commit sin anymore thereafter. Thus, your life must be sin-free **always.**

A deliverance worker must be able to diagnose the type of evil spirits he is dealing with; thus, whether he is dealing with demons, human spirits or any other unidentified or disguised spirits. To know your opponent gives you the opportunity to get it from Jesus Christ whether to lay charge first and counsel thereafter or vice-versa; and the strategy to apply relevantly.

Important: Do not attempt deliverance or its counseling if you are not delivered yourself or assist ushers in this process, or if you do not have enough time to complete this task.

If the assistance of ushers will be necessary at a long run – it must be of ushers trained in handling such cases; or otherwise nobody should be around except the deliverance team at the maximum of at least one to three members only.

The room at which this process is taking place should be restricted to the team members only; and the latter should, not disrupt the process; but must stay focused until they decide to terminate the undertaking.

Counseling must be done sequentially in order of human-structural-personality-development or form trying to identify areas mostly forming satanic strongholds; starting from the spirit man, soul and flesh.

Try to isolate covenants from curses; and both from sins. Be careful that sins may never form part of the actual deliverance session, but a person may be given chance to confess and repent from his/her sins and be tried first before attempting deliverance on him. A record of individuals counseled should be kept in order to keep pace with the Holy Spirit to be able to recall each person's areas of captivity when approval is gained to perform such on the person.

Very important: Never try to perform deliverance on anybody unless otherwise the Holy Spirit confirmed to you to proceed. The same applies even in counseling – if God commands you to stop the counseling session; please do that immediately. The reason is that God knows the future and He cannot subject anybody to a doom. A person must be ready and understand that he is not worthy to commit sin anymore thereafter but is apt to lead a holy life forever.

Who should be assisted with deliverance?

Any person who accepted Jesus Christ as his personal Savior (meaning a person who accepted salvation) and has been baptized according to the way of salvation as spelled out in the baptismal of John the Baptist. The person must be willing to get deliverance after receiving thorough teachings on deliverance; and must understand that he is still a captive even though he has committed himself to Christ. He must also understand the concept of being-born-again and holiness as the only way of survival.

The following *guiding table* can assist you to cover all the areas in a person's life in order of captivity. Usually, if the spirit man is under bondage, there is no way the physical body and soul can be free. Please note points of concerns under every section that constitute man; and indicate a positive mark (+) or a negative mark (-) where applicable:

Key: (*) critical point; (+) captivity; (-) clear and no evidence of bondage

Spirit (predominantly covenants)	**Physical body (predominantly curses)**	**Soul (predominantly affective)**
*Being named after *Speaking to the dead *Baptismal from other religions *Initiation schooling *Contact with spirits *Consultation with the mediums and spiritists' *Astral projection *Idolatry *Practice of yoga *Engagement in martial arts *witchcraft *Engagement in ritual practices *Occult practices *Devil activism (practice of Satanism)	*fornication *Premarital pregnancy *Rejection *Abuse of any form *Vagrancy *Death at young age *Divorce *Poverty *Illnesses *Cannibalism *Lust *Procrastination *Pornography	*Anger *Bitterness *Hatred *Unforgiveness *Worry *Depression

How to use the guiding table

- Explain to the counselee the type of questions you are going to embark on. (*Thus, he/she has to relax and feel free to participate*) some questions are easy to understand and answer, while others are somehow difficult and sometimes embarrassing to be reflected upon.
- Begin by isolating any form of captivity on part of the spirit as spelled out in the table above under the heading 'spirit.' (*it is not necessary to follow the sequence on the table*) the portion reflects mostly on covenants applicable.
- Make sure you get the details of events if known to the person being counseled, and that you understand what you have been told.
- All positive (*things that the person being counseled became engaged in*) marks reflect the type of covenants established, and their form of engagement. You can therefore find out about the severity of engagement – this may indicate the degree of possession.
- Find out about any physical engagements the person has, as spelled out on the table under the heading 'physical body.' The positive marks you get reflect the type and forms of curses inherited and those established.
- Please make sure to follow the **genealogical history** of the person with regard to every item spelled out in the table above.
- Take into consideration that most of the items may be biphasic – thus they are curses or covenants, which originated primarily as sins committed. Therefore, assist the person to ground off such, by teaching them to ask for forgiveness and repent their sins. This will make any demons or evil spirits that follows such a channel to have no grounding or inclination as a stronghold.
- Items under the heading 'soul' are a mere reflection of the operation of demonic spirits riding over a person's spirit man and become reflected as emotions that are usually exaggerated, and usually influence the individual behavior.
- Make sure not to get confused by similarity of events during counseling.

- This table only helps you to have the insight of what you must look for, but the Holy Spirit is there to keep you through.

NB. The spirit, physical body and soul constitute one man and should therefore, never be perceived as entities because every covenant, curse or sin affects the entire being.

Examples:

- If a person is *being named after* another; say for instance after his grandfather; he is definitely going to carry along the blessings and the curses of the latter and lead his life the same way as his grandfather did. Thus, if the owner of the name (*grandfather*) was an abuser and suffered divorce – the whole package becomes attached to the successor and apt to suffer the same way. Merely because the name forms part of the active-covenant and keeps networking between the new owner of the name and the kingdom of darkness.

  Therefore, one is advised to be very cautious when giving names to one's children; and has to understand the origin and the meaning of each name before naming his/her children.

- *Fornication* and all other sins of the same classification are bi-dimensional in the sense that it is classified as sin – and can be forgiven if the person can confess and repent of it. However, its second part, which is classified as curse remains with the person as long as it is not broken by means of deliverance. Therefore, the generation of such a person shall carry the curse of *rotten relations* through all of its roots. Please take note that every sin committed opens a doorway for the free entry of demons and evil spirits.

- *Anger* is a feeling and a reflection of the emotional state of a person at a given time. Under normal circumstances, this applies to every body and differs according to the degree of severity. An acceptable anger reflects sensible mind with soberness; with the ability of an individual to exercise conscience and discern between the right and the wrong – and be able to do the right even if angry.

Nonetheless, in the case of captivity – things turn around during this state; irrespective of the degree and period because the real person fades off and evil spirits take-over and ride on the mind of a person like a dark cloud.

He/she becomes determined and extra-energetic to cruelty. After completing the devil's will the evil spirits go away temporarily and leave him alone to face shame. This condition is so innate to such an extent that a person be classified as fragile in emotions or an element of hostility. This is one sign of bondage where a person needs the mercy of God for his/her freedom.

Dealing with the sins

A person should be assisted to accept that he is a sinner. This is the only way to survive the initial step through submissiveness and obedience; moreover because many people are declared holy according to the worldly order and some have classified them worth of credit before the Lord. This is why spiritual growth is impartial on their account because they deny the truth in the word that:

1 John 1:8
If we say that we have no sin we deceive ourselves and there is no truth in us.

It takes the mercy of God for one to reach this stage of acceptance for one's weaknesses and come up being ready to confess such in prayer to God and to man in sharing.

James 5:16
So then, confess your sins to one another and pray for one another so that you will be healed. The prayer of a good person has a powerful effect.

However, many people start to marvel during the process of deliverance when the Holy Spirit reminds them about the sins they committed that are up to so far not forgiven. Many of them begin to realize that they assumed to be good before the Lord, whereas they were just deceiving themselves and relaxing in a deadly paradise.

The safe and best way to access, a promising state of affairs is to regard oneself not worthy of the Kingdom of God in true sense, but being given the opportunity only by **Grace.**

Romans 3:24
But by the free gift of God's grace all are put right with Him through Christ Jesus who sets them free.

It is the spirit of deception that drives-in the feeling in people that they are in good standing with the Lord for them to relax and assume that their battle is over and that they definitely will inherit the treasures of Heaven.

May I highlight it to you dear reader that it is true that God is holy and no sin or inequity shall be found in Him. His ways are more than our perceptions and His thoughts are more than magnificent. He is indescribable.

Matthew 7:21
Not everyone who calls me 'Lord, Lord' will enter the Kingdom of heaven, but only those who do what my father in Heaven wants them to do.

The only remedy, which is up to so far available for the treatment of sins is the sacred blood of Jesus, which only comes into effect when the sinner confesses his sins and begs for forgiveness and cleansing thereof.

Ask the Holy Spirit to let you know about any sins you committed that has not been forgiven. You should embark on a prayer and fasting at least for one full day. Have a paper and a pen to right all those sins as being spelled out to you by the Spirit and if you think your memory can serve you well, you need not write anything. Brown (1990, p. 188 – 195) outlined the following the steps below to assist in self-cleansing:

The format of dealing with sins and self-cleansing:

- Pray and ask for the forgiveness of each sin in the name of Jesus Christ (*1John: 1:9*).
- Pray and ask to be cleansed with the blood of Jesus for each sin (*1John 1:7*).
- Thank the Lord for forgiving and cleansing you of your sins. (*Hebrew 11:1, James 1:6 - 8, Isaiah 1:18 - 20*)
- Take authority over all evil spirits and demons, which entered into you through any channel of entry, cast and bind them all out, in the name of Jesus.
- Close each doorway in the blood of Jesus and **never commit sin anymore.** Sin will open doors for demons back into you, and each open doorway will draw in all other demons and evil-spirits, back into or invite others, which may be more powerful than they may.
- Have faith that all your sins that you presented before the Lord are forgiven, and finally destroy the paper that you scribbled on (*Isaiah 1: 18; James 1: 6 – 8*).

NB. Never commit sin anymore!

Important: Certain sins require more effort to get the doer completely cleansed of them. For an example – if a person has stolen something from someone, he/she has to bring back the stolen items to where they belong and pend the consequences thereafter; or if the above effort is impossible due to whatever reasons, all the stolen items should be brought to the deliverance team and be destroyed.

NB. Nothing should be left. No matter how good or valuable the item may look to the person; but because it is stolen, it carries with it the plaque of the stolen item – and therefore a curse.

Please make sure not to attempt assisting a person with deliverance without having cleared all the areas of captivity accordingly; otherwise, whatever is left behind will remain a **trap** and an open portal of entry for the demons and evil spirits, which makes an unclosed channel and an active link with the kingdom of darkness.

Therefore, if the above situation cannot be properly dealt with; that person remains a captive and liable to the kingdom of darkness indefinitely.

Remember we are dealing with the person who has accepted Jesus Christ as his personal savior; and who really needs to be a born again child of God.

Preparation

The next step after having completed and exhausted every spell in digging for the areas of captivity from the individual; is getting ready for the actual day of deliverance and the preparation is as follows:

The deliverance worker:

- Make the Bible your friend. Read it every day and make sure you understand the interpretation of the scriptures as meant.
- **Don't sin.**
- Maintain high standard of fellowship secrecy – never divulge any information you got of a person, lest you will be disqualified in the ministry of deliverance.
- Pray and fast every week for at least a day, two, or more. *(NB. Do not fast at the day you are going to work to avoid body weakness, because you may need some energy and strength to complete the work. Deliverance is strenuous and taxing.)*
- Have enough time for a "**Quiet Time**." A quiet time is time spent in meditation of the "**word**" and listening to revelations of the Holy Spirit in every aspect He may deem fit to reveal to

you. Be sensitive in listening otherwise you may miss important information and blunder.

- Make sure you understand what has been interpreted to you before acting, or else pray and ask the explanation from God on what He said to you.
- Establish with God for the people on your list about their readiness and the one who should be assisted first before the others.
- Please do not use your discretion but let the Holy Spirit guide you. Remember this is a spiritual battle and you are not the one determining the fight – but Jesus Christ.
- Be alert for any traps coming your way and be a winner.
- Don't feel ashamed or scared to postpone assisting a person with deliverance if you are told that he/she is not ready for it. Because what is the use of assisting a person with deliverance, who will thereafter go back to his/her previous sinful state willingly!
  Rather keep counseling him/her and assist him/her to reach relevant maturity level before you proceed. Some people may take longer than others to get ready for deliverance, but it is not your business – wait for God to guide you.
- Fervently, pray always for those people who have come afore to your assistance. Pray for their protection and security in the blood of Jesus; and pray that they have mercy before the eyes of the Lord.

The following hints may be useful to you

- Have some red meat to gain enough strength. You need to be physically fit to handle different cases. (1 Kings 17:6)
- A 100% pure grape juice may help sooth your gastric ulcers if you suffer from any. (This may result as retaliation attack to you – most intercessors suffer from such discomfort. (1 Timothy 5:23)

The place of work

- A successful deliverance should be conducted in a room meant for such work only.
- Preferably, a place should be within a church setting – and not a public place meant for many other activities.

Matthew 9:25-26
But as soon as the people had been put out, Jesus went into the girl's room and took hold of her hand, and she got up. The news about this, spread all over that part of the country.

- It must be quiet and free from interferences.
- There must be a provision for bath or shower with towels *(this will help those people with demons manifesting with **rolling** and **jerking**; or **snaky** movements to have bath thereafter to maintain their cleanliness).* Avoid any sort of embarrassment to the person you help, maintain his/her dignity. **Do not** even testify to other people about him/her.

A person to be assisted with deliverance

- Should be on prayer and fasting on his/her day of deliverance if it is a scheduled one.
- A female person should bring along some slacks to wear before the process. This is to prevent nudity because demon spirits manifest in deferent ways; and are apt to bring shame to divert the focus of deliverance workers *(be very careful because many deliverance workers fail, and are highly likely to become possessed themselves at this point).*
- Provide facilities for shower, as it may be necessary for the counselee to take a bath after the process to maintain personal hygiene. (Some people may roll on the floor or vomit etc during the prayer). Remember to maintain personal dignity of individuals at all costs.

The following are the demonic manifestations in a person; and usually differ according to individual captivity; thus the degree at which each person is possessed and the spirits in place. A person can be possessed primarily, intermediately or become fully engaged in Satanism:

Signs of a primary possession

A person may still be harboring demons while no obvious evidence is observed; and might not be knowing about his/her status but may reveal during counseling, some bizarre behaviors he/she discovered of him/herself. When being prayed for – he/she may display the following:

- Cough – a person may cough profusely when he had no cough beforehand.
- Sneezing
- Yawning
- An urge to urinate / defecate
- Nausea and sometimes vomiting
- Sweating is common even when there is no strenuous activity performed.

Signs of intermediate possession

In one way or the other; there may be a known history of the period of possession or his elders may know of something that was done upon him earlier or during birth.

- Screaming – an evil spirit may scream as it comes out or as it is tortured.
- A person may be fighty or tries to run away
- May complain of heat or burning as the name "Jesus" is mentioned
- Seizures may be common.
- The behavior is entirely evil.
- May display stubbornness
- May have spells of sleep-walking

Signs of advanced possession

In this case, a person knows everything about his/her covenant with the devil to serve him. He/she is a **Devil Activist (DA)**, and usually participates in accordance with multiple powerful demons that give him power to do miracles and wisdom to know.

Apart from demon possession, there might be a possibility of **Human Spiritism** that should be outlined in order to know on what basis is your fight so that relevant strategies may be applied:

- Being taken off (a *petit mal* picture) thus, falling into a trance while in action. This is very common in this category.
- Communicating with the spiritual world using gestures or verbal cues including speaking in tongues (*Never be deceived demons can fluently speak in tongues and mimic the presence of the Holy Spirit – while they proclaim terrible curses)*
- Battling – they do not usually give up easily. Fighting back physically when being prayed for is a common manifestation. (*Remember it is not the person you are helping who is fighting you, but a vast army of evil spirits in backup)*
- Amnesia (*forgetfulness*) – is a strategy usually used to dilute the progress and to frustrate the counselors and let them give up.
- Confusion – this is a double standard – play, to confuse the counselors. NB. *Never let this condition persist if you observe it manifesting because if it may be ignored, it may render that person permanently psychotic.*
- Playing normalcy – A person may behave as if there is nothing wrong with him/herself; and may display signs of good character of Christianity to gain acceptance and favor among the believers.
- Knowledge of the scriptures – (*it only depends in which category the person is; some may be inclined to preaching – only to distort the truth in the Bible.)*
- A person may roll from side to side; be jerky (a *grand mal* formation) or display a snaky movement depending on types of evil spirits

possessing him/her or all of the above mentioned manifestations might be displayed.

NB. The above manifestations may not be the sole criteria to diagnose possession because evil spirits are so vigilant to despise at any given point; therefore consider every thing serious and never let any stone unturned!

The actual deliverance

- Remember to start all the sessions with prayer earlier before you begin.
- Pray for the people you work with; your relatives; friends and neighbors; and every body else on earth for protection in the blood of Jesus.
- Pray and seal the place of work with the blood of Jesus.
- Important: remove anything in the room which may be used as a weapon e.g. bottles, knives, sticks, bricks etc.
- Bind all the traps and evil spirits around in the name of Jesus and burn them.
- Make sure that it is either early in the morning or in the afternoon – otherwise you are going to get exhausted waiting for the ancestors to wake up and listen to the person's confession if it is during midday.
- *(An active covenant requires the second party to get rid of it – which in this case is the devil and all his agents. Assist the person to proclaim against it)*
- If the person is saved – begin by assisting him to break all the covenants and the curses identified in the guiding table during counseling *(render all null and void in the name of Jesus.* **Never leave anything behind.** (*Allow the person to follow after your words and make sure that he says exactly what you said he/she must say)*
- Listen to the Holy Spirit carefully. Apply "*waiting for the Lord*" strategy. This will help you keep pace with Him and get it right the first time.
- Because you are in a fight, the demons in a person may obtain a backup – but will never reach beyond the seal you established

earlier on in the blood of Jesus. *(Unless you have active sins yourself– therefore be pure before the Lord)*

- You may experience their presence when they arrive because they come-in full of rage and disturbed in their programs; but because you know – please don't panic but do all in the name of Jesus for the sake of the captive next to you.
- During the process, sing praises and worship songs that contain the words *"the blood of Jesus"* – this will help you end the battle quickly and successfully.

* * *

- After completing the above phase – let the person proclaim blessings upon him/herself and his/her children, possessions and finances, environment and every aspect identified as a curse during counseling. *(Lead him/her as during the process and allow him/her to speak after you)*
- Finally, lay hands, pray for the person for protection, and bless him/her. Make sure not to pray for anybody before breaking his/her covenants and curses.
- NB. Warn him/her never to commit sin anymore. If he/she sins you have no part in that; and refer:

  1 John 3:8-9
  Whoever continues to sin belongs to the devil because the devil has sinned from the very beginning. The Son of God appeared for this very reason; to destroy what the devil has done. **None of those who are children of God continue to sin; for God's very nature is in them**; and because God is their father they cannot continue to sin.

* * *

- The next very important item usually omitted is the cleanup of the person's environment. After completing the work of deliverance successfully consider any item available; which the person possesses and is an element of theft in any way and destroy it by burning it with fire.

- These items you wouldn't know as a deliverance worker, but he/she will inform you if they are available or not. Warn him/her not to spare any stolen items or those used in connection with witchcraft, other religions etc. Their presence in his/her environment breaks the "seal" of protection to his/her belongings and makes them vulnerable for burglary and free flow of demonic spirits.
- Prayer-walk the environment and proclaim the name and the blood of Jesus and fire to set up a "permanent seal".

* * *

- If a person is not saved – there is no way he can be delivered. Rather assist him/her profess his/her faith in Christ by accepting Jesus Christ as His/her Lord and Savior.
- In addition, if a person is a Devil Activist – consider exorcising the evil spirits first and win his/her soul to the Kingdom of Light. Train him/her intensely about the word of God and bear in mind that backsliding is imminent in such people because of the threats imposed upon them by Satan.
- Be careful that you cannot drive a person out of Devil Activism if he/she is not willing to quit especially if he/she is in high ranks of the cult.

Finally, as a word of advice, deliverance is laboring and it needs one to have passion inspired by the Holy Spirit to survive the ministry and to fulfill the will of God about the gifts of the Holy Spirit at hand.

Life during deliverance (the battle zone)

It should be indicated clearly to the person seeking deliverance that the moment he/she seeks deliverance marks the beginning of the battle. The battle intensify because the demons know very well that they are going to loose habitation and their kingdom is about to loose a member. Therefore, they wrestle to win him/her to the state of captivity. The person must be warned to be watchful about the type and frequent attacks manifesting because the demons influencing a major attack represent the stronghold in a person. For example, if anger is the major stronghold of demons in a person, there will be instances, which frequent anger practices to that person to bind him/her further, to prove that he/she cannot survive a holy life.

Again, one cannot claim to be a winner without having engaged in a war and win over his/her opponent. Meaning, for survival, such battles are tests to be passed and not failed. If a person fails a test, he/she surely must write it again, and if he/she cannot pass the tests is the more he/she is going to take long in deliverance without getting approval of the Holy Spirit to survive life after deliverance. Therefore, do not ignore, but warn the person about experiences such battling more to breakthrough.

Life after deliverance (the maintenance zone)

Life post deliverance is endless engagement with the Lord. A season of Holiness, which requires determination to serve the Lord, now with understanding and commitment – it is only through serving with understanding a person can remember his/her covenant with the Lord. Prayer life, obedience and humility are the only tools to keep the lamp burning.

The deliverance workers should have seasonal meetings with the community of delivered people to allow them time to share their experiences and ventilate their concerns, and to give further lessons as a way of nurturing. It may be one-on-one meeting with the counselor or a group meeting. People must be encouraged to participate in different ministries of confirmation and to timeously, engage in scheduled prayer sessions.

Challenges facing people during maintenance zone

Importantly, at this stage somebody who finished deliverance successfully is a number one enemy of the kingdom of darkness. Therefore, he/she becomes battled against day and night without rest. The common attacks are not found away from the work and place of worship. The following are few examples to mention:

- Pride and Arrogance – post deliverance, people may find themselves too holy to interact with other people. They may face tests such as self-exaltation and undermining their superiors, even people who helped them grow to that level may be subjected to disrespect. Therefore, be careful not to fall a victim of this deadly sin.

* * *

Tele-Acquittal (Remote Deliverance)

Tele-acquittal or **Remote Deliverance** (*Matthew 15: 22 – 28*) is a form of intercessory prayer, which is meant solely for delivering individuals, environments or situations in a purpose of setting them free of evil spirits infestation. It is done normally once active possession is evidenced either in behaviors or in actions or history of individuals whose access is impossible or if circumstances are impermissible to arrange a meeting with them and is in dire need of deliverance according to the deliverance worker's assessment. The Holy Spirit must confirm to you that deliverance is an option of choice to remedy the person, environment or situation.
This type of prayer may be done at a sole discretion of a deliverance worker after confirming active possession. The **on-scene** prayer can only be done for people who are at easy reach, and after a counseling process is completed.

The focus of this type of undertaking is merely to attend to the three components of a human being namely the flesh (body), soul and spirit. The intercessor should aim at forcefully driving out evil spirits in a person targeted and those influencing from outside his/her body and the source, bind and destroy them in the name of Jesus. The knowledge of specific areas and possible class of demon spirits operating in a person is very crucial to focus on during this type of deliverance.

Deliverance workers know that they are normally challenged by such evil spirits when they feel an attack, therefore doing a complete job will spare you from such retaliation attacks.

Some of the people or their environments in this type are implanted with items that serve as telecommunication devices in their bodies. These items are open communication channels between the person/environment and the kingdom of darkness just like the way an artificial communication satellite works. Destroy such items and their link in the name of Jesus. If such items are not destroyed, the person's life will just be a vicious circle and may soon die. You need to seal that person, environment or situation with the blood of Jesus (you just proclaim).

If you make this type of prayer to a person whom you can access, you may try to introduce the knowledge about Jesus Christ to him/her or use another person to do this for you. Be very careful about your approach or else never attempt it in any way. You can simply send him/her Bible scriptures, invitations to prayer meetings etc.

Never loose hope on his/her part, Jesus Christ is the one who is doing the whole job.

NB: If you ignore them, they will die permanently in hell.

In conclusion:

John 8:31-32
So Jesus said to those who believed in Him, "If you obey my teachings you are really my disciples; **you will know the truth and the truth will set you free."**

CHAPTER 11

Almost Over

Jeremiah 29: 13
You will seek me and you will find me because you will seek me with all you heart.

For so many times in our life we come across different developmental stages towards becoming full-grown with relevant knowledge for our spiritual age just like a growing child from infancy to adulthood. It is due to reasons such as this that we have to be given enough chance to grow and attain a state of being 'perfect and complete, lacking nothing' so that we are able to stand all trials without failure (*James 1: 4*).

From the scripture above, we can understand that it matters a lot to God to see to it that our wellbeing is catered for. That, even during times of hardship He is there to fulfill His promises upon us, and that if He wants to mould and position us correctly as He wills, it is not a problem to Him to subject us to any form of punishment as long as we can be corrected. It rest upon us to understand the love he has for us. The position of God to His children is just the same as the way our parents are, to us as their children. A parent, who matured from different aspects of life, is always positive towards grooming his/her children towards independency of their future life. This can be by giving positive advices, rebuke, lessons or imposing some sort of punishment to indicate the seriousness of the matter at hand and to demonstrate perfect love to the young ones. Truly, where there is no love there is no form of caution, but where love is abundant, there is curiosity accompanied by jealousy to see the safety and wellbeing of one's children secured.

For this reason, since it is our must to believe that we do not know God, and on His ways, we stumble because of ignorance and lack of knowledge, we therefore, have to understand our standing and vehemently strive to seek knowledge about Him.

In the book of Jeremiah chapter 46 verse 28, the Bible records ***"... I will not let you go unpunished: but when I punish you, I will be fair. I the Lord have spoken."*** In so many times we fault and go astray of His will, He remain patient to guide and to teach us through His word, but we remain adamant to realize that it is Him who is taking charge over us. By the time He subject us to punishment as a certain form of reprisal to His word to remind us about Him and repent we still do not recognize the message.

God is Love with a bond that is so strongest to detail perfection. He does not entertain any rivalry but requires obedience to His will. The Will of God is a key to enter the Gates of Heaven (*Matthew 7: 21*). Jesus stated it clearly to His disciples that the only way to unlock the gates of Heaven is by doing the will of God. If we can have a clear meaning of this scripture and understand fully how we have to go about unpacking the mode of operation to accomplishing it, then we have it. It is clear that it will not be by the works and the great deeds we do that we can be acceptable, but by doing the Will. Therefore, the main question that remains to be answered is 'how to do the will of God?' Do we do the Will of God basing on the conditions we stipulate our self and how much consistent are we in giving honor to His name in things He give us opportunity to do without putting our name first?

Our state of ignorance about the Will of God is so bad that we usually opt to forge what we think it is the Will and begin to put the conditions for us and align them to His will. This is the main tool the Devil is using to reap out knowledge and prevent people from attaining this necessary knowledge. Instead of seeking for the truth, it is all contrary and to the worse.

Lies and false interpretation of scriptures is a weapon made to destroy all the necessary knowledge about God. However, knowledge is of no use if it does not benefit the knower. Being able to talk much about the scriptures and to interpret them fluently is a benefit, but what does it matter if all the knowledge we have is impracticable and remained just a theory to the knowledgeable?

It is high time dear reader that we should mind our eternity. Time is now not in our favor; we need to repent and fully commit ourselves to knowing the Lord and make certain that our relationship with Him is not just a shallow one. There is just this little time left, little as just a volume of breath we inhale in a given fraction.

If we mind, as much about our eternal life, we would lead our remaining time of life as if we are told it is all over, because there is no tainted soul that will be allowed to appear before God. Not deceiving ourselves, we need to, truly seek the face of the Lord in this regard.

The first step we should consider is to clean ourselves spiritually, and to be so sure that we do the cleaning process genuinely without deception. This must be accomplished through prayer, confession of our sins and a belief that what we put to the Lord in prayer is heard and answered. The type of prayer for situations as this should be done without doubt in order to be successful.

The point of failure emanate from the dubious attitude we have when making our presentations to the Lord. The fact that we cannot see God physically serves as a tool to destroying our sincere faith to His existence and interventions in our life issues. This is to the extent that we resort to believing and putting our trust to things we see and can easily access, and invoke God's anger.

Our attitude to God, as far as faith is concerned, should be the same as siblings' faith to their parents. *Firstly*, read the Bible and meditate about the scriptures to seek understanding so that you are deep-rooted in the Word. *Secondly,* strive to practice what you learnt from the Bible – it is a good thing – and encourage yourself to push on and stick to the good until the good become your habit. *Thirdly,* strive so hard to eradicate all the bad habits and attitudes you know about you. Nobody will fight your battles unless you do it yourself. People may just come and back you up with their prayers, but a winning urge relies on the fighter him/herself.

Moreover, God use situations, trials and people to communicate with us. Just be alert to Him, be acquainted with the means of communication directed to you in a point, and make certain you understand the message or otherwise remain inactive until you know what and how to do if you have to act.

The main issue is the Will and then other things follow as the results of the seed implanted in our spirits. The Will and only the Will of God is the one major factor above all human intentions and wisdom.

Actually, what is the Will of God? The question may seem ridiculous and sometimes self-explanatory, but truly, it is not. Concerning the scriptures, we sometimes assume that we understand, but we only realize the difficulty with our understanding when we have to practice according to the Word. It is at this point, where the misunderstandings brought about a lot of confusion, where different interpretations emanate to further, lead us far away from the connotation of the author's context.

Yes, it is allowed to have different interpretations, but not all the interpretations are correct as spelled out in the Bible. Our focus should be to strive to get the undertone of the author and have a contextual and operational view of the scripture concerned and before we make additions that confuse us more.

The Will of God is simply the Word of God, and the Word of God is achieved through thorough and analytical study of the scriptures and empirical research by allowing the Holy Spirit to guide the proceedings in all these approaches. For decades, and over many generations, people struggled to fully, come to terms with the actual goal about the ministry of

Jesus on earth. The purpose of Jesus' ministry is to liberate the captives from captivity and set a platform for redemption of the souls for eternal life under the covenant of 'Blood.' It is not for the physical comfort as we assume and proclaim through contemporary evangelism, as it is commonly uttered.

The Bible records in the book of *Matthew* 6:33 (KJV) that "*but seek ye first the kingdom of God, and His righteousness; and all this things shall be added unto you.*'This scripture outlines the purpose of the ministry of the Lord, but the adversary has brought in the interpretation to otherwise, seek first these entire things and the kingdom of God shall follow. This is how it is seen and heard in many teachings where preachers embrace wealth and achievements as a sign of blessings than to emphasize the way of righteousness to eternity. Our Father in Heaven knows our situations, predicaments, all the joy and even setbacks that we go through. He uses such encounters to spruce us and set us ready for the Kingdom so that we may not forget Him and perish.

To cite an example, go to the scriptures in the book of Acts and realize the persecution the Apostles underwent or a bit back to some of the prophets. Even today, people who stand right in the Lord are suffering the same fate; they become victims of their fellow worshipers who resist against them such that they give-in. Anyway, Jesus prophesied about these, that:

Matthew 23:34
And so I tell you that I will send you prophets and wise men and teachers; you will kill some of them, crucify others, and whip others in the synagogues and chase them from town to town.

It therefore remains clear that these are the end-times where signs are obvious to proclaim the Bible prophesies. To those who care about their eternal life, it is time now to make the final checks and put everything right with you for the Lord is about to appear in the sky.

In conclusion

Revelation 22: 12
"Listen" says Jesus. "I am coming soon."

Chapter 12

Death

The Dictionary meaning of the word 'death' is said to be the total and permanent cessation of all vital functions of an organism (Dictionary.com, Online). By virtue of understanding, death is the most feared encounter, which most people do not even want to hear anything about. However, it is one of the topics, which has drawn more attention in many religious literatures as well as in the Health Care fraternity. The author of this book is of the opinion to include some text as far as this topic is concerned to pose a scriptural view and to present another dimension regarding the way it is perceived.

Death like pain is perceived in different ways among individuals, but pain is better because it has some relief depending on the type and cause. Unlike death because once experienced it means a point of not coming back. The Bible outlines two types of death. The first is death due to cessation of breath and bodily function resulting into lifelessness (*1Corinthians 15: 20*). The second is the outcome that determines eternal destination of souls after the judgment (*Revelation 20: 6; 14*).

- **Death in the first place**

I refer to this type of death as a common form of separation of soul and the flesh, with a perception that there was no word such as 'death' during the life in the Garden of Eden until such time that Adam and Eve wronged. Death, however, originated as a form of punishment to human race (*Genesis 1: 19*), but was later on transformed to become a good messenger, which unites man and his Creator (*Romans 5: 10*). By the way, no one can live forever in this life, but people need to come, act and pass on to give space to others. It becomes clear that this type of death enables a person who dies in the Lord to rest upon his/her works. What matters the most according to the phrase above is - it depends on whether death occurs when the dying person is in good standing in the Lord or away from the Lord. If the dying is in the Lord, it means joy to the person who dies because he/she is going to rest in his/her good works.

However, if death occurs to a person who is not in the Lord that is where the trouble begins upon the dying:

Revelation 14: 13 (KJV)
And I heard a voice from Heaven saying unto me, write, blessed are the dead which die in the Lord from henceforth: yeah, saith the Spirit, that they may rest from their labors, and their works do follow them.

- **Death in the second place**

The issue of the second death will come out as a final condition, which will subject over those who cannot make it through the judgment and those who will be found unworthy of Heaven. However, since there is no second chance to make corrections on the wrongs (unconfessed sins) one committed once dead – it means a license to overcome the second death is doing the right things in this life. Meaning, gaining favor of God to qualify eternal life is simply abiding in Jesus Christ.

John 5: 24

I am telling you the truth: those who ***hear my words* and *believe in Him who sent me* have eternal** life. They **will not be judged, but have already passed from death to life.**

The scripture is self-explanatory and clears all the other myths about the destination of souls after death. The souls of the righteous will at no stage rest in the grave, not after the resurrection of Christ the Lord. Those who are made righteous by the Lord never assemble for judgment during the judgment day because they would have already made their way to Heaven (a great promise). There are categories of people who will not be found among the multitudes during the judgment day. The first category is of the people mentioned in the scripture above, and the second category has two divisions in it as outlined in the following scripture in Psalm 1 verse 5, which read as follows:

Psalm 1: 5 (KJV)

Therefore, the **ungodly shall not stand in the judgment**, nor **sinners in the congregation of the righteous.**

To bring closer the understanding about the occurrences of the final day (judgment day), let us liken the situation to our normal judicial proceedings where a criminal will be arrested and kept into prison until the day he/she appears in the court of Law for questioning and testifying before a sentence can be passed. The judgment passed is normally based on the evidence found during investigations prior to the court date.

The souls of people who died unrighteous (ungodly) never go to Heaven as we may so wish, but are kept in Hell to await judgment there. By virtue of understanding the scriptures, Hell is a prison where souls of people who died sinners are held captive while awaiting the final Day of Judgment. The categories of the dead in Revelation 20: 13 (*then the sea gave up its dead. Death and the world of the dead also gave up the dead they held)* are those whose souls are in hell.

To summarize, **in spirit**, the **dead in the sea** are the 'ungodly' as it appears in Psalm 1 verse 5 above. They are those who dedicated themselves to serve Satan and who have sworn to die eternally; the example of such is the 'werewolves.' **Death and the world of the dead** cover the souls, which are held captive in Hell (mostly sinners who died before repenting from their sins).

The Lake of Fire

Let us be careful that Hell and Lake of Fire are two different places with different purposes. Hell is for souls awaiting trial, and The Lake of Fire is a place of final destruction of Satan, False Prophet, Antichrist and all those who followed and served him (*Revelation 20: 10*).

Important: let us examine the following scripture

John 5: 25
I am telling you the truth: the time is coming – the time has already come – when the dead will hear the voice of the Son of God, and those who hear it will come to life.

It sounds ambiguous to try to understand the meaning of this scripture, but let us recall the scripture in the book of Matthew 27 verse 52 and 53 and realize that this part of the scripture was fulfilled and may not be confused with any scripture pertaining the judgment day.

The dead

The scripture in Ecclesiastes 9 verse 10 outline the difference between death and the souls of the dead in relation to the physical participation to the living. It emphasizes the inability of such souls to participate in life again. Be it the souls of the righteous or the wicked, the scripture refer to both categories so that we have clarity and get rid of myths that lead to confusion to worship the souls of the dead.

However, the four categories of evil spirits spelled out in the book of *Ephesians 6: 12 (for we are not fighting against human-beings but against*

- ***the wicked spiritual forces in the heavenly world,***
- *the **rulers,***

- ***authorities** and*
- ***cosmic powers of this world)**,*

are responsible for advancing communication between people and the spiritual world. The most common means of communication is **dreams** to the relatives of the deceased, **hearing of voices** giving instructions to their victim claiming to be god and sometimes **ghostly-appearances** to their target. Never listen nor obey their instructions, torments or bribery, but rebuke them in the name of Jesus and they will flee.

Important, the separation of soul and body (flesh) is usually what is termed clinical death. The body (flesh) is buried in the grave or cremated etc. according to different cultural practices of people on earth. However, irrespective of the type of death a person underwent, the Apostle Paul stated in the book of 1Corinthians as follows to indicate the imminent reunion of body and soul at the coming of Jesus Christ:

1Corinthians 15: 39
and the flesh of living beings is not all the same kind of flesh; human-beings have one kind of flesh, animals another, birds another and fish another.

The body (flesh) of human beings is designed to resurrect (*John 5: 25; 1Corinthians 15: 42*) and never to decompose permanently wherever its remains are, but to wake up from the dead, reunite with its soul, transfigure (*1Corinthians 15: 44*) and to face judgment (Revelation 20: 13). However, the context of the Apostle in these scriptures is mostly focused on the saints and as a word of encouragement to keep their faith in Christ.

The corpses of the just in the graves and elsewhere will rise first and be transfigured to take a spiritual form and be ready to meet the Lord (*John 5: 25*). They will rule with Christ for thousand years (*Revelation 20: 4*); and can never be affected by the second death, for they will never go for judgment. Those who will still be alive by then (*and are righteous*) will also be transfigured into a spiritual form never to die.
Likewise, the corpses of the unjust will also rise after a thousand year of Christ reign (*Revelation 20: 5*), at the sound of the trumpet, but to rise

for shame (*John 5: 29*). Thereafter, the following scriptures will then be fulfilled:

1Corinthians 15: 54
So when this takes place, and the mortal has been changed into the immortal, then the scripture will come true: "death is destroyed; victory is complete!"

Revelation 20: 14
Then death and the world of the dead were thrown in the lake of fire (this lake of fire is the second death).

Hell and death together will be destroyed by fire because there will be no prisoners' anymore-pending judgment, and all evil will be destroyed from the universe.

The Bible did not hide any truth about the destination of the souls of people after death, it spells it all clearly, but we need critical analysis of the scriptures and guidance of the Holy Spirit to reveal these truths.

God bless you!

In conclusion

Revelation 22: 17
The Spirit and the Bride say, "Come!"

Printed in the United States
By Bookmasters